Loving Your Children Better:

Matching Parenting Strategies

To the Age and Stage of Your Child

Loving Your Children Better:

Matching Parenting Strategies To the Age and Stage of Your Child

Mary Ann Little, Ph.D.
Kevin W. Karlson, J.D., Ph.D.

Westport Publishers, Inc.
Kansas City, MO

Cover design: Noelle Kaplan, finedesign

ISBN 0-933701-53-5
Library of Congress Catalog Card Number: 90-72034

Printed in the United States of America

In fond memory of Donna Kaelson Little

Table of Contents

Part Two

Acknowledgments

There are many people to thank.

My friend and colleague, Kevin Karlson, first encouraged me to write my ideas down. His organizational help, writing, and energy were essential.

In the early stages of this project, many friends and colleagues read manuscripts and offered valuable criticism and conversation. My thanks to Jerry Lewis, Byron Howard, Joan Berger, Paul Chesmore, Barbara Otto, Diane Funk, John Tatum, Lee Usnick, Patricia Rose, and Michael Coleman.

I owe special thanks to Nancy Bray who carefully read and re-read chapters at a moment's notice, generously giving time that she did not have. Her uncanny common sense and good judgment helped to clarify many sections of the text. In addition, her gentle friendship and commitment to my work sustained me through this lengthy process.

Special thanks also to Marty Brown who read and critiqued almost every revision of the manuscript. His comments were always wise and helpful, but his enthusiasm for my ideas provided important comfort during the difficult periods.

Perhaps most importantly, I give my heartfelt thanks to Susan Steadman who in many ways deserves to be a co-author. Her gift for words and clarity of thought are evident in every page of this book.

Finally, I thank my husband who believed in me and this project and my children who lived through the process.

This book, like others of its kind, is the product of many people's work. I have tried to acknowledge the influential writings in the bibliography. My Piagetian thinking stems directly from my years as a graduate student under the direction of Judy Keith, Jane Raph, Beth Stephens, Barbel Inhelder, and of course, Jean Piaget. My psychoanalytic thinking and knowledge of developmental psychology come from more traditional academic sources, interaction with my colleagues and work with my clients. The ultimate product is a synthesis of many models, but the final responsibility throughout is mine.

Mary Ann Little
Dallas, Texas
1991

Part One

Introduction

Part One of *Loving Your Children Better: Matching Parenting Strategies to the Age and Stage of Your Child* provides parents with an overview of the developmental approach to interpreting and dealing with children's behavior. As the information is applicable to all children from birth through adolescence, we hope that parents will read Chapters 1 through 4 before proceeding to the chapter in Part Two which deals specifically with their child's developmental stage.

In Chapter 1, we describe the basic premises of this book: parents must have knowledge of child development; parenting strategies must change over time; parents must differentiate normal developmental occurrences from problem behaviors; and parents can learn to be better parents.

Chapter 2 explains how the course of development is similar for all children. We will reassure you that development is discontinuous in nature; that is, set-backs and interruptions are to be expected. In Chapter 3, we talk about how parents sometimes unintentionally erect roadblocks to their children's healthy development. Finally, Chapter 4 takes a close look at three essential elements in a child's development: feelings, thoughts and actions.

1

Loving Your Children Better

As wonderful as it might be to imagine, parents do not suddenly undergo some magical transformation at a child's birth which allows them instinctively to know all there is to know about children's development. In fact, understanding children—especially, understanding how to discipline them—is a special art with its own unique rules and principles. And if the job of parenting were not difficult enough to begin with, it is complicated by the fact that these rules and principles change over the span of childhood. Interpreting a child's behavior with sympathy and compassion may mean one thing when that child is a toddler, and something quite different for the same child during a later developmental period. Therefore, a parent's decision about what to say or do about that behavior must change as well.

The Journey

Parenting, then, is one of those seemingly simple issues that is, at heart, impossibly complex. It continues to baffle the best educators and psychological experts, to say nothing of well-meaning parents. Part of the problem stems from the difficulty of being objective about children you love and with whom you live.

Throughout the ages, the task of rearing children has been both praised and scorned. In their attempts to describe its joys and frustrations, writers have compared parenting to virtually every known human experience. Regardless of one's sentiment on parenting, metaphors offer the potential to illuminate this subject.

To help in the process of understanding childhood development in an objective way, we have decided to compare the developmental process to traveling, since traveling is an activity that virtually all Americans know something about. In a real sense, this journey is one made by both the child and the parent; therefore, we will refer to aspects of this journey variously from the child's perspective and from the parent's perspective. We hope that the "journey" metaphor will encourage parents to step back a bit from the crisis of the moment and look at the big picture. Finally, the idea of traveling communicates that the process of helping children grow up healthy is one that takes time and involves a number of different stages and phases.

Premise #1

Parents Must Have Knowledge of Child Development

This book focuses on the inner workings of children in an attempt to help parents understand and love their children better. Our goal is to prepare you to respond effectively to your children's communication and behavior. While most child clinicians understand children from a developmental perspective, efforts to share professional information with the lay population have often been subject to misinterpretation. This book strives to make the tenets of developmental psychology applicable to the practical problems of child rearing on a day-to-day basis.

The importance of a developmental perspective cannot be underestimated. Many books which we have reviewed approach parenting from a static point of view, assuming quite erroneously that children are miniature adults with limited intellectual capabilities. These books therefore derive parenting models (that is, ways of dealing with children's behavior) which remain constant over time. We have found, however, that the same techniques may not work at different stages of the child's development nor for different levels of misbehavior. In contrast to many other parenting guides, then, this book argues for a "Developmental Discipline" approach. Because children transform as they grow, parents' management techniques must shift to accommodate developmental changes.

In general, developmental psychology attempts to describe and explain childhood behavior, showing how what happens in early childhood helps shape children as they reach later stages in their lives. In addition, developmental psychology demonstrates how the same behavior in different individuals may stem from very different causes. For example, one adolescent who seems to have no time for intimate relations may just be concentrating exclusively on academics for a period, while another teenager who has no close friendships may actually fear intimacy. In other words, all seemingly identical behavior does not mean the same thing.

A developmental perspective emphasizes that there is a process of normal development. If you can learn about this process, you can provide responses, experiences and information for your children which help with all the necessary steps along the way as they grow up and mature.

Premise #2

Parenting Strategies Must Change over Time

As we have stated, children change as they grow, and therefore, to be effective, parenting strategies must also change to suit the child's current level of development. While this fact may seem obvious, in our practices we have seen a surprising number of parents who have adopted a single-minded, unwavering plan. So much has been written in the popular press about the importance of consistency in parenting that parents have often mistakenly assumed that you must always treat a given behavior in the same manner.

In addition to the need for changing strategies according to the child's age, there are two other modifications of the "consistency" guideline to keep in mind. First, you can be consistent without being absolute. For example, a child's playing on the kitchen floor with a truck might be fine most of the time, but *not* when you are preparing (or the family is eating) dinner. Second, a particular rule can change from situation to situation. For example, a child may be prohibited from eating snacks in the living room at home, but invited to do so at Grandma's house.

In short, although there is no doubt that consistency in parenting is important (indeed, we will use the term ourselves in describing effective parenting techniques), translating "consistency" into rigidity may result in serious negative consequences for both parents and children.

In what we hope are simple and concrete terms, we discuss the various stages of child development and offer advice on which parenting strategies are likely to work with children in those stages. We also single out the management techniques which we feel are likely to prove most successful in a given period and those that may be helpful but are not the preferred choice.

While specific principles will be detailed in later chapters of this book, our general philosophy can be summarized as follows: **discipline for young children should involve consistent behavioral responses as they learn best by experiencing the natural consequences of their actions.** For example, children will learn that time is an important concern if they find that not being ready at two o'clock means that they miss a playmate's birthday party. They will recognize that their parents' instructions are meaningful when they discover that leaving the gate open means that the dog gets out; that not putting clothes in the hamper means a uniform is not ready when needed for the soccer game; or that leaving their math homework on the desk at home means they get a zero from the teacher.

With the very best of intentions, many parents protect young children from the natural consequences of their behavior. Unfortunately, "protecting" children this way deprives them of the vitally important learning experiences whereby they come to know that their behavior really does matter, and that the consequences of this behavior are predictable. Significantly, such protection subsequently interferes with the development of feelings of mastery and basic security in the world. Children who are protected from consequences in early childhood are forced to learn some fundamental truths in adolescence when the consequences are far more injurious and much more risky in terms of the child's emotional growth. **If parenting in early childhood has helped children learn through the use of natural and nontraumatic consequences, parents can then enjoy the luxury of parenting through verbal negotiation and logic as their children enter adolescence.** By this time in development, children have acquired the cognitive or intellectual maturity to control their behavior by adult-like reasoning. Discussion and compromise can then be the primary parenting techniques.

In our experience, many parents have adopted parenting strategies that are the precise opposite of those proposed in this book. Too often, parents attempt to control their youngsters' behavior through reasoning or logical discussion. This strategy is doomed to failure because small children do not yet have the cognitive ability to understand or appreciate their parents' efforts. For instance, many parents ask preschoolers *why* they did what they did, not realizing that at this point motivation is irrelevant to the situation. When "Why did you hit Jimmy?" produces "Because he took my crayon," where is a parent to go from there? Such exchanges end in total exasperation for the parents. After all, the child's answers don't excuse the behavior; the reality is that the child should not hit, no matter what.

Unfortunately, the situation deteriorates as the parents grow more and more disturbed by their children's inability to respond to their management attempts. In the worst case, some parents resort to harsh punishment with extreme consequences in late childhood or early adolescence, just when a child has acquired the ability to reason and is finally capable of responding to parental logic. Through lack of information about child development, a terrible mismatch has occurred between parenting style and the child's level of maturity. Such an error can jeopardize the parents' and child's potential for being friends when the child reaches young adulthood. It can leave a child feeling traumatized and unloved, and parents feeling victimized, frustrated and incompetent.

Premise #3

Parents Must Differentiate Normal Developmental Occurrences from Problem Behaviors in Order to Devise Appropriate Management Strategies

As we have repeatedly emphasized, parents need a certain amount of knowledge in order to make informed decisions about the meaning of a given behavior in their child. This determination is very important because it essentially dictates what is an appropriate parental response (and what is an inappropriate one). Although later chapters of this book will spell out the distinctions among different types of behavior in greater detail, we would like to present some general guidelines here.

A parent must make a decision about whether a behavior falls into one of three categories: **normal developmental occurrences, routine behavior problems** or **serious behavior problems requiring professional attention.**

Normal Developmental Occurrences

The first question to be asked is whether a behavior is to be expected during the normal course of development—is it a "mile marker?" Generally speaking, if a behavior grows out of an area of particular interest or upset which is to be expected at a given age, then we consider it to be a normal developmental phenomenon. A good example is a child's reaction to an unfamiliar adult. For a seven- to nine-month-old baby, a fearful response is quite normal and should be met by appropriate comfort and nurturing. This "stranger anxiety" in a four-year-old is *not* an expected response; careful consideration and decision-making will be necessary in determining how to handle the behavior.

Another example is curiosity about sexual differences. In a five- or six-year-old, questions and behaviors (such as playing "doctor") that illustrate this interest are quite normal. You should be prepared to give comforting and thoughtful answers to difficult questions and perhaps gently deal with some mildly inappropriate behavior. However, a similar preoccupation in a nine-year-old child will probably require very different management, as it is not a normal interest in this stage.

In summary, not all similar behavior has identical meaning, nor does it require the same parenting techniques. Fortunately, scientific research in the field of developmental psychology specifies anticipated behavior during different phases of childhood. In later chapters we will summarize that research and outline what is normal and expectable for children in the various stages of development.

A behavior is also considered a normal developmental occurrence if it results from an emotional upset that causes the child to act more immaturely than usual. Consider this sad example arising from a parent's inability to differentiate normal developmental stresses from routine behavior problems and to devise specific strategies for each. A well-meaning mother had read several parenting books and decided upon a "time-out" procedure for her four-year-old son's tantrums. This technique, which involved placing the child for a short time in an area where an activity he desired was unavailable, had worked well for a while. Regrettably, she utilized time-out when the boy began to cry uncontrollably after the family dog chewed the raggedy ear off his favorite teddy bear, a toy which he had slept with since infancy. In this mother's attempts at consistency, she sent the child to time-out in his room for his tantrum, thus missing an important opportunity to love and comfort a child who had experienced a significant psychological loss. Extreme reactions to loss are normal in small children and should be met with understanding and patience. In this situation, it was appropriate for the parent to help a child soothe himself by providing soft arms, a gentle voice, and sincere efforts to repair a valued possession. **You need to remember that what a child experiences as traumatic may seem insignificant to an adult.** Moreover, strange as it may seem to parents, very different kinds of events may have great psychological significance to a child. A pet's serious illness, the father's out-of-town business trip, and the failure of watermelon seeds planted by the child in the backyard to sprout—all may be equally upsetting to a five-year-old.

A third consideration in assessing normal developmental occurrences is whether the child is under such significant stress that behavior regresses (i.e., retreats to an earlier stage of development) or changes in some undesired fashion for a more extended period of time. For example, a little girl whose parents were in the midst of a divorce and whose housekeeper was leaving the family at the same time might display noticeably more aggression on the playground. This aggression, extending over several weeks, may be punctuated by episodes of tears over perceived criticism from the teacher or slights by her classmates. Here again, taking the child to task for her oversensitivity or misbehavior would be clearly inadvisable. Instead, extending additional support and attention would be the strategy of choice.

Again, normal developmental occurrences may be the result of developmental interests and/or conflicts, a function of a real-world "insult" (the term for a psychological injury that accounts for an extreme behavioral response), or stem from an overall period of stress that causes behavior to deteriorate for a duration.

We recommend that you be supportive when normal but difficult or unpleasant developmental occurrences present themselves. You can make serious errors by failing to see a child's behavior within the framework we have offered. Traditional discipline measures for stage-expectable or stress-produced behaviors are clearly unwise and can have profound negative consequences for your children.

Routine Behavior Problems

To a certain extent, the term "routine behavior problems" identifies behaviors that are neither considered normal developmental occurrences nor viewed as the serious behavior problems described in the next section. Rather, they are "potholes in the road"—the kinds of irritating behaviors that bother parents on a daily basis. A few examples include a child's failure to come to dinner when called, incidents of minor aggression with other children, name-calling, unwillingness to complete certain chores, or mild lack of respect for adults.

We want to stress that any topic we treat as a routine behavior problem could be considered a serious behavior problem warranting professional consultation if its form is unusually intense or if it occurs over a long period of time.

In general, we recommend that you use different behavior management strategies during different developmental phases. Our overall premise is that younger children require more behavioral and immediate sorts of strategies such as positive rewards or time-out, while older children require more discussion, compromise and problem-solving—approaches which may entail lengthy discussion or family meetings.

Routine problem behaviors require consistent parental responses. That erratic attempts to deal with undesirable behavior can lead to unfortunate results was exemplified by a family whom one of us recently saw. In an effort to avoid their child's disappointment and subsequent unpleasant behavior, the parents would often gratify his every wish for weeks on end. At the age of five, the child was allowed to select any toy he desired his parents to purchase for him and to decide what he would eat at mealtime. The parents soothed every sign of distress in their son and did not allow him to experience any frustration (even what we would consider appropriate frustration); nor did they utilize effective strategies to manage his tantrums. Periodically, the parents would reverse themselves and take a harder line, refusing to give in to their son's whims and engaging in disciplinary measures, only eventually to return to their former indulgent responses and lack of limit-setting. The end result was the boy's inability to deal with daily frustrations. He hit children who "beat" him in games. He yelled when his teacher selected other kids for classroom jobs. Failure to provide limits on a consistent basis impeded the youngster's development; he failed to learn many coping skills that are an absolute necessity in life.

Serious Behavior Problems

The third class of behaviors covered in this book lies outside the realm of either normal developmental phenomena or routine behavior problems, and requires professional consultation. In each of Chapters 6 through 10, we provide a brief list of serious behavior problems (ranging from extreme phobias to cruelty to animals to drug abuse) which cause the journey to be "stopped on the road," and warrant special concern. In addition to these lists, **we encourage you to consult with your pediatrician, educational specialists and/or mental health professionals if you have any questions.**

Obviously, a parenting strategy which does not differentiate between normal developmental occurrences, routine behavior problems and serious behavior problems is faulty. Any misunderstanding or lack of knowledge that hampers a parent's ability to make these distinctions can lead to trouble for a family.

Premise #4

Parents Can Learn to Be Better Parents

The final premise of this book is that most parents can learn to be good parents and that good parents can become even better parents. After years of work in our respective clinical practices, we have become convinced that the majority of parenting mistakes grow out of insufficient information about normal development in children, and not out of a lack of concern or good intentions. As a result of parents' inadequate knowledge, children are misunderstood by the very people whose love and respect they most desire and whose signs of frustration and seeming lack of regard have the most profound consequences.

It is indeed unfortunate that our society has not provided better ways of disseminating information regarding child development and parenting. In our estimation, this failure is partially the fault of professionals who have not made scientific information available in a highly practical way. The current popularity of parenting handbooks simply indicates the need for such resources.

Theoretical Influences on "Developmental Discipline"

Several distinctive approaches have contributed greatly to the creation of this work, and many of their theoretical notions are interwoven in the material presented here. We wish to acknowledge the substantial influence of these major theorists or schools of thought on our thinking and the book's organization.

The following list is not intended to be exhaustive but to highlight the most significant sources in a necessarily highly summarized and simplified manner. We refer you to works dealing specifically with each of the following for more detailed information. The bibliography contains a number of useful sources.

Jean Piaget and Cognitive Theory

Piaget, a famous Swiss psychologist, made major contributions to the study of intellectual growth. He saw the child's development as an attempt to make sense of the world by dealing actively with objects and people. He determined that children go through sequential cognitive stages, with each stage building upon the earlier ones, until they can reason logically and abstractly. His work, which stimulated interest in maturation as a key concept in intellectual development, emphasized the importance of cognition on many other aspects of psychological functioning. He hypothesized four stages of intellectual growth: **sensorimotor** (birth to 18 months), **preoperational** (18 months to age 7), **concrete operations** (age 7 to 12), and **formal operations** (age 12 onward).

Sigmund Freud, Erik Erikson and Psychoanalytic Theory

Freud was concerned with how individuals reach or fail to reach the goal of emotional maturity. For Freud, maturity meant the adult's ability to cast off childhood conflicts and to love another human being. Freud saw the child as passing through successive, age-related stages, each of which revolved around a different body part. Thus, infants pass through an **oral stage**, toddlers, an **anal stage**, preschoolers, a **phallic stage**, and adolescents, a **genital stage**.

Adapting Freud's system, Erikson delineated specific developmental tasks throughout the entire life span. His theory focused on the interpersonal aspects of **growth** and **development**. According to Erikson, psychological growth occurs in a series of stages with successful learning at each stage laying an increasingly solid groundwork for later stages. He outlined the developmental phases as follows: basic trust and affiliation vs. mistrust, independence and autonomy vs. shame and doubt, initiative and assertion vs. fear and guilt, industry vs. inferiority, identity vs. diffusion or role confusion, intimacy vs. isolation or self-absorption, generativity vs. stagnation, and ego integrity vs. despair.

Learning Theorists and Learning Theory

In contrast to Freud and Piaget, learning theorists focus on overt behavior without emphasizing cognition, feeling, or desire. Emphasizing the influence of the environment and of reward and punishment, they tend to deny the impact of maturation and are unconcerned with stages of development. Learning is viewed as the process by which behavior is modified and as occurring through conditioning and/or observation. **Classical** or **operant conditioning** involves the pairing of a given behavior with a set response (for example, a baby turns her head and is given a bottle). **Observational learning** is acquired by watching the behavior of others.

Lawrence Kohlberg and Moral Development Theory

Kohlberg investigated moral development in children and adults. He was not concerned with the content of moral judgments but rather with the rationale the child or adult used in making those judgments. He identified **successive stages.** Very simply put, children move from making moral decisions based on the avoidance of punishment and the achievement of awards through a stage based on the avoidance of disapproval and maintaining the law, and into a stage dominated by a concern for social contracts and for ethical issues.

How Best to Make Use of This Book

Chapters 2, 3 and 4 are devoted to the basic tenets of childhood development. In keeping with our journey metaphor, which reinforces the idea that the developmental perspective defines an ongoing process, we describe children's developmental journeys as featuring mile markers (consecutive phases of growth), areas under construction (critical periods), flat tires and potholes (interruptions in development), and so on.

In Part Two, Chapter 5 outlines the many management strategies available to parents, each of which is appropriate in one or more periods, while Chapters 6 through 10 cover the separate developmental stages. Although these stages are not, strictly speaking, determined by the chronological age of the child, for purposes of simplicity they are divided here into typical age ranges for each predictable developmental level. However, we want to stress that some children will be advanced for their age and some children will be behind. In other words, chronological age provides only a rough index of the probable level of development at which a child functions. Individual differences will result in deviations from the outline and age ranges used here. (Both your pediatrician and your child's teachers can provide you with an idea of the child's relative acceleration or delay, should you need some reassurance.) The phases are listed below:

- **Ages birth to two—Infant Years:**
  Structure Phase (Chapter 6)
- **Ages two to four—Toddler Years:**
  Choices Phase (Chapter 7)
- **Ages four to seven—Early Childhood Years:**
  Rules Phase (Chapter 8)
- **Ages seven to eleven—School Age Years:**
  Agreements Phase (Chapter 9)
- **Ages eleven to eighteen—Adolescent Years:**
  Reasoning Phase (Chapter 10)

We encourage you to read Chapters 2 through 4 very carefully as they contain basic principles applicable to children of any age. Afterwards, you should proceed to the chapter designated for the child's age range.

Chapters 6 through 10 are organized as "trouble-shooting" guides. The first section of each chapter identifies the **normal developmental processes or mile markers** and typical behavior during the period. The second section outlines **recommendations for preventive maintenance**—the specific steps you can take to aid your child's normal development. The third section contains **specific behavior management strategies for staying on the road** which we have found to be most effective for each developmental phase. The fourth section describes **routine behavior problems** that are likely to arise during each period—the **potholes in the road**—and offers practical suggestions about managing these problems through do-it-yourself tune-ups. Finally, the last section of each chapter deals with more **serious problems which warrant a call for help** or professional consultation.

Our Hopes for Your Journey

One of us recently heard a funny story that expresses our hopes for this book. A little boy was asked by an adult what he wanted to be when he grew up. The boy replied, "I want to be possible." Intrigued and puzzled, the adult inquired further, "What do you mean?" The child explained: "My mother says I'm impossible. When I grow up, I want to be possible." This book is our attempt to help parents raise "possible" kids and enjoy the process of doing so.

2

Mile Markers Along the Road: Basic Concepts in Human Development

The road to development is neither straight nor smooth for any child. Rather, each individual's route from birth to maturity more closely resembles a winding country lane, wide and smooth in some spots, narrow and rocky in others, with numerous potholes and detours along the way. This chapter is about the normal bumps and expectable detours which occur in every child's journey from birth to maturity.

One key to understanding children involves the concept of developmental stage. Anyone who observes children will soon notice that as they grow, children change in all ways: physically, intellectually, psychologically and emotionally. What may not be so obvious is that all children go through similar stages in each of these areas.

Because individual children grow at different rates, age is not a reliable indicator of a child's developmental stage. In other words, two children of identical ages may be facing different challenges. Developmental psychologists have discovered sets of developmental tasks which all children must accomplish in order to continue to grow. In contrast to physical growth, where failure to grow is readily apparent, failure to accomplish the developmental tasks for any given stage will not completely halt the child's maturing, but rather interfere with continued normal growth.

For example, an important task in the period between 18 and 36 months is the development of autonomy: the ability to separate from the mother (or primary caregiver) without undue distress, to be reunited with her without difficulty, and to play independently in the meantime. One requirement for healthy development during this phase is the ready availability of the mother to the toddler. If for some reason the mother is not available, perhaps due to an extended hospitalization, the child may find subsequent separations difficult for a long time, even if the mother returns from the hospital safe and sound.

In adolescence, a major developmental activity involves exploring and establishing relationships with members of the opposite sex. Should the teenager have to deal with the trauma of his or her parents' divorce during this period, progress in forming such relationships may be hindered.

That children's behavior is indeed variable, subject to inconsistencies, uneven development and unavoidable detours, is underscored by the multitude of parenting groups sprouting up all over the country. Not surprisingly, parents want reassurance about the normal boundaries of behavior. How comforting for parents to find that they are not alone in facing the hard task of deciding when to be concerned about their children's development and when not to be.

Mile Markers are in the Same Order for Every Child:
Development Unfolds in an Unchanging Sequence

Development follows a sequence which is the same for all children, with new skills and abilities building on those which the child has already acquired. Even though some children proceed through the stages faster than others, the stages which we will identify cannot be skipped by any child. In other words, in the absence of a serious developmental problem, each child passes through every level.

The process by which children amazingly layer new ability upon new ability has been termed the principle of "hierarchical development" by developmental psychologists. You might visualize this as a pyramid.

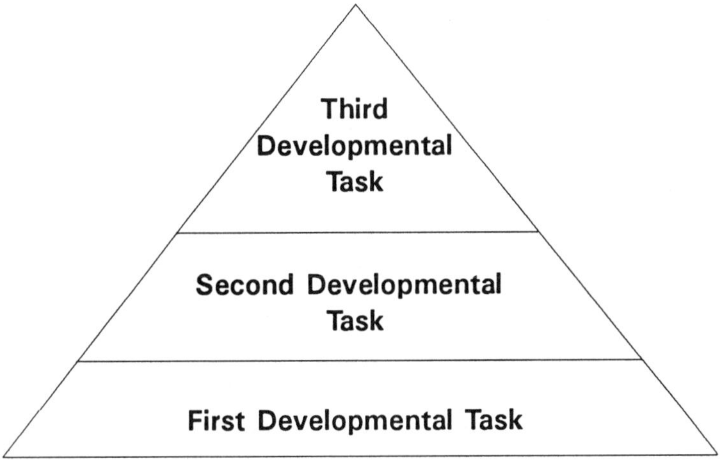

The unchanging sequence of developmental stages appears to be the same for all children, regardless of race or culture. What does vary, however, is the speed at which individual children proceed through this sequence and how far they will ultimately go.

5 Miles Per Hour Today, 100 Miles Per Hour Tomorrow:
Development is Discontinuous

Children pass through periods when they seem to be changing right before your eyes, and other periods when they seem to be frozen at some level of development. The figure below graphically represents children's uneven developmental progression.

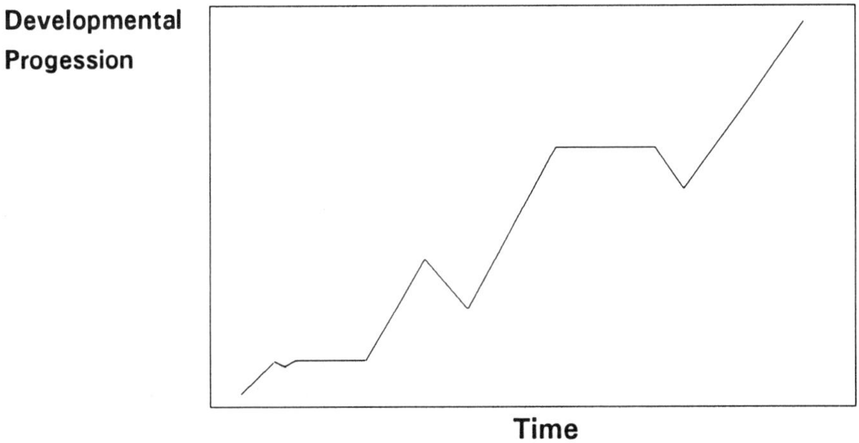

Accelerated development in young children may prove a mixed blessing. A child who is walking by nine months may be the source of pride for her parents as well as the cause of considerable consternation since anything within arms' reach is likely to find its way to the floor or into her mouth.

We should mention that accelerated motor development does not necessarily mean the child is gifted, and average motor development does not necessarily predict average IQ. In fact, a rather large body of research has found that precise predictions of children's IQ before age six or so are generally unreliable.

Delayed development is more significant in young children (under age five) than is accelerated development. Any delays should be discussed with your pediatrician. In some cases, the physician may recommend a formal evaluation by a psychologist, speech and language pathologist, audiologist, physical therapist (for large motor skills) or occupational therapist (for small motor skills).

Children develop at their own pace. Comparing developmental milestones may be interesting, but we caution parents about interpreting differences in the time at which they are reached.

It is only when children appear to be six months or more behind their peers in achieving developmental milestones during infancy and early childhood that parents should usually consider a professional evaluation.

One example of a common, harmless developmental delay is seen in some youngsters who do not develop language as early as their peers. Parents of such children begin to worry that their babies will never talk. Then, one day, to the parents' great delight and astonishment, these children with no apparent vocabulary begin to speak, and within a few of weeks may be on a par with others their age.

Caution—Child Under Construction:
Critical Periods in Development

It is obvious to even a casual observer that children do not develop everything at once. At certain times, different tasks come to the fore and assume top priority for the child, and then recede into the background. These times of intense focusing on a particular developmental capability are called "critical periods" or "times of increased susceptibility."

Just as embryologists have discovered critical periods in prenatal development (for example, a pregnant woman's exposure to German measles in the first trimester may produce birth defects in the fetus), psychologists have found that psychological development is also sensitive to critical periods. An important example is a young child's language development, which seems to undergo a critical period early in life. Failure to develop language comprehension or production skills at this time results in language problems that may be difficult to fix. This is evident in children who have physical illnesses, such as recurrent ear infections, during this critical period. Chronic fluid build up from ear infections can disrupt language and speech by interfering with the child's ability to hear adequately and therefore to mimic accurately.

Another example involves the reproduction of speech sounds. Most children are born with the ability to mimic the sounds of any language. If exposed to and rewarded for producing certain sounds—those of the child's native language—the child's oral mechanism begins to specialize in that language and loses its ability to mimic unfamiliar sounds. This phenomenon accounts for the relative ease small children have in pronouncing foreign words and the relative difficulty adults experience in acquiring and mastering a foreign "accent."

Other noteworthy critical periods, which we will discuss in the appropriate chapters, include ages 18 months to three years, when children undergo the process of psychological separation from the mother, and ages four to six, when children establish sexual identification.

A Flat Tire Means You Have to Stop:
Development Can Be Interrupted

Not only can interruptions take place in any child's development, but an interruption in one avenue of growth will likely influence other areas as well.

At one extreme, some victims of severe child abuse and neglect have been found to suffer from a disorder which prevents normal physical growth and intellectual development. Thus, in addition to the emotional trauma which they have suffered, they are also very short and underweight when compared to their peers, and below average on intelligence tests. This condition, which results from undersecretion of an important growth hormone, can be reversed by removing the child from the abusive situation. Physical and intellectual development often return to the normal range.

In the same way that complete deprivation can disrupt normal development, so can too much help and protection. While "spoiling" children is not a consideration before the child is able to walk and talk, children must undergo some frustration in order to develop properly. Furthermore, they need to experience the natural consequences of their actions in order to learn. Children who do little for themselves soon expect the world to take care of them, and become helplessly dependent on others and very demanding. Overgratification as well as undergratification at any stage of emotional development seems to freeze development at that point, and interferes with further maturation and independence.

Parents need to distinguish interruptions in development from delays in development. Children who have been maturing normally before experiencing some difficulty in one developmental stage have probably suffered a setback which has interrupted their growth in some sphere. For example, a five- or six-year-old who has already established her independence from her mother and is doing well in kindergarten, may suddenly refuse to attend school when her mother becomes very ill. The girl's behavior may even backslide to that of a three-year-old, because she has experienced a traumatic event which served as a developmental "insult." (As you may recall, an insult is a psychological injury which accounts for an extreme behavioral response.) On the other hand, a child who is slow in learning to count has not lost that ability, but simply never developed it, despite opportunity and instruction.

Potholes in the Road:
How Development Is Interrupted

Any event in the life of a child may bring about enough distress to cause a temporary interruption in the course of normal development. Many occurrences are very upsetting to children even though they appear insignificant to adults. Because children have neither the cognitive nor emotional maturity of adults, they are much more easily affected by seemingly minor happenings. A change from morning to afternoon kindergarten, a small toy accidentally being flushed down the toilet, or even taking an ill pet to the veterinarian is each potentially stressful enough to disrupt briefly a child's ordinary progress. The importance of events like these to a child depends upon his or her perception of what happened and understanding of why it happened, as well as the emotional significance of the event. Those factors are in turn heavily influenced by the child's developmental stage.

A large body of research has established that change is stressful. For adults and children alike, more change means more stress. In other words, the experiencing of more than one change (stress) at a time produces disproportionate upheaval. A move to a new home, a death in the family, or a change of teacher may each, if experienced in isolation, be tolerated far better than if the child is faced with them all at once. This is why psychologists suggest spacing out potentially stressful situations if possible. It would not be abnormal for a child who has undergone a serious illness and the arrival of a new baby in the family at about the same time to show signs of interruption in development and even appear to have lost some previously acquired skills.

Not surprisingly, the event which is most likely to be stressful to a child and prove to be a developmental insult is the death of a parent. For children younger than school age who live in a traditional household, the death of their mother will probably be more traumatic than the death of their father.

At the other extreme, even relatively minor changes in daily routine may lead to temporary interruptions in development. One of us recently saw a three-year-old whose abrupt changes in behavior had led his parents to seek professional help. In contrast to his previous behavior, Tim was having trouble interacting with other children, refused to go to bed at night, acted finicky about eating and was generally negative in reaction to parental requests. The parent interview revealed that Tim's primary caregiver had recently been replaced by a new caregiver whose work schedule required a change in sleep and meal times for the child. On top of that, the family had just moved. Once additional support was given, Tim's unusual behavior abated, and the parents were reassured when he returned to normal in a couple of weeks.

Research into the effects of stress on children has resulted in the creation of a scale of stressful occurrences. The scale printed below, taken from Dr. David Elkind's *The Hurried Child,* illustrates the relative impact of some events on children. Larger numbers indicate greater stress for the child.

Death of a parent	100
Parents' divorce	73
Parents' separation	65
Parent's traveling as part of job	63
Death of a close family member	63
Personal illness or injury	53
Parent's remarriage	50
Parent's being fired from job	47

Mother's going to work	45
Change in health of a family member	44
Mother's becoming pregnant	40
School difficulties	39
Birth of a sibling	39
School readjustment (new teacher or class)	39
Change in family's financial condition	38
Injury or illness of a close friend	37
Starting or changing an extracurricular activity	36
Change in number of fights with siblings	35
Being threatened by violence at school	31
Theft of personal possessions	30
Change in responsibilities at home	29
Older sibling's leaving home	29
Trouble with grandparents	29
Outstanding personal achievement	28
Move to another city	26
Move to another part of town	26
Receiving or losing a pet	25
Change in personal habits	24
Trouble with a teacher	24
Change in hours with a babysitter or at daycare	20
Move to a new house	20
Change to a new school	20
Change in play habits	19
Vacation with family	19
Change in friends	18
Attending summer camp	17
Change in sleeping habits	16
Change in number of family get-togethers	15
Change in eating habits	15
Change in amount of TV viewing	13
Birthday party	12
Punishment for not "telling the truth"	11

When a child accumulates more than 300 total stress points in a twelve-month period, the parents can probably expect a change in either the child's health or behavior, or both.

Backing Up to Take Another Run at the Next Hill: Developmental Regression

Regression is the term that psychologists use to describe the process of temporarily losing ground along the developmental journey. Parents are sometimes frustrated when Johnny, who could channel a spoon to his mouth every day for a week, suddenly cannot even seem to hold the spoon. Such regression in motor skills is a normal part of early childhood development.

Regression can occur in other realms as well. A youngster who has developed the ability to stay with a babysitter without crying while his mother is away for a couple of hours, may suddenly become very clinging, and not want to separate from her at all. This is a regression in the child's capacity for independence, and will occur many times during the course of normal development.

Cognitive (intellectual) development is also prone to regression, as exemplified when children "lose" a problem-solving skill they have already mastered. A preschooler who has learned to count to ten may from time to time be unable to count, or may get some numbers out of sequence. Inconsistency is an inevitable part of the process of mastery.

Regressions are usually caused by an event which temporarily exceeds the child's ability to understand or cope. The event could be a change in the child's daily schedule or diet, or a shift in the mood of the caregiver. The key to understanding a regression is to find a change in the child's environment which has demanded some adaptation by the child. Whatever the cause, regressions are most often a normal part of development.

We do need to add a word of caution, however. Some regressions may signal a physiological problem, such as a brain tumor or disease state, and therefore demand that the parent seek professional consultation. While such cases are very rare, any parental concerns should be investigated.

Sports Cars, Sedans and Station Wagons: Temperamental Styles Affect How Children Act

Children are born with a certain "temperamental style" that is classified into one of three groups. Stella Chess and Alexander Thomas, a well-known research team, have studied differences in children's behavior which are evident even in newborns. They observed that children's temperament falls into groups which they called "Easy," "Difficult," and "Slow to Warm Up." Evident from birth into adulthood, these styles appear to be relatively unaffected by external influences. A child's temperament seems to place biological limits on a child's physiological reactivity and sensitivity, and on the quality of his or her interaction with others. Although temperamental characteristics are constitutionally based, appropriate handling by parents is essential.

"Easy" children are the ones every parent hopes to have. These children quickly adapt to a schedule after birth, are not prone to excessive crying, are quickly soothed, snuggle when picked up, and generally induce great confidence in their caregivers. As they grow older, they are more likely to be socially outgoing, relaxed, pleasant people.

In contrast, "difficult" children are a challenge from the first few days of life. These children cry frequently, are hard to soothe, and seem not to enjoy cuddling, often becoming rigid when picked up. They are overly reactive to noise, lights and changes in temperature, are easily overstimulated, and prove extremely frustrating to their caregivers. As these children grow older, parents, teachers and other observers continue to rate them as more irritable, energetic and volatile than "easy" children.

"Slow to warm up" children are those whose characteristics fall in between the other two groups on most dimensions. They tend to be less adaptable than the "easy" children, but less reactive than "difficult" children. The major distinguishing feature is their ongoing preference for easing slowly into situations with unfamiliar people, tasks and activities. They are cautious, and even as adults may appear somewhat reserved.

One example may help to clarify how temperamental style can interact with developmental stage. Imagine the difference in the three groups of children as they reach the "terrible twos," a period in which youngsters become increasingly independent and "No!" is a favorite response. At this stage, children appear alternately clingy/dependent, and oppositional/independent. For the parents of "easy" children, this phase may pass almost unnoticed, as the children shift smoothly back and forth from dependence to autonomy. Power struggles will be infrequent, and interactions between parent and children remain low-key and usually pleasant. Life with "difficult" children can be more challenging than ever during this phase. "No" may seem to be the only word in their vocabulary. They may seem unhappy when alone, and unhappy when held. Minor changes in routine or diet may lead to major confrontations or "digging in their heels." The behavior of the "slow to warm up" child will fall somewhere between the other two. For these children, separations will be less traumatic, yet reunions with parents less warm and spontaneous. They establish their independence, but with less persistence, and they are more easily diverted.

A Few Small Dents Will Not Affect How Well The Car Runs:

Children Are Resilient and Parents Do Not Have to Be Perfect

Parents often need to remind themselves that children have proven to be very resistant to damage by parental omissions and misjudgments. While it is important for you to be consistent over the long haul, day-to-day variations in understanding, patience, and nurturing are to be expected, and will not hurt your child in the long run. The cumulative effect of good parenting will outweigh the impact of minor parental errors in judgment.

By the same token, when disasters strike a family, parents may have difficulty coping, too. At these times, children are not harmed by expressions of feeling by a parent. Children learn by example. When they see their parents crying over the death of a loved one, they learn that sadness is a natural consequence of loss, and that crying can be a healthy emotional release. If children are frightened by these expressions of emotion, they can be reassured with a hug and a straightforward explanation, such as: "It's all right. Mommy is sad because she misses Uncle Joe. Sometimes when people are very sad, they cry for a while." Such experiences not only are not detrimental, but will be very beneficial to the child later on.

Even when you demonstrate an inappropriate loss of control, such as an isolated incident of screaming or slapping a child, it is unlikely to be harmful unless it occurs regularly. Parents need only be concerned when they find themselves repeatedly screaming at their children or hitting them whenever they are upset. At that point, professional help is imperative, both for the child's emotional development and for the parent's emotional well-being. (Such intervention is necessary for a minority of parents and children.) In addition, some parents find particular ages very difficult to deal with and may benefit from professional consultation to smooth out the trouble spots.

In most cases, children seem to turn out okay regardless of the parents' skill—or lack of skill. Parents should realize that it is not necessary to be a model parent every minute of every day in order to raise psychologically healthy children. A temporary "regression" in parents' approach to managing their child will not undo a history of positive, consistent parenting. Adapting a few of the skills outlined in this book will likely make a good parent a better parent, and may help make a normal child an even healthier, more confident child.

We hope that our discussion of the detours along the road to development has increased your appreciation of the incredible variation among children in how they develop. At the same time, you should be able to recognize that the process of development is very similar for all children, once the signposts and mile markers are familiar. Our goal is to make the journey easier for parents and better for children.

3

Roadblocks to Normal Development

In an ideal world, the journey from birth to maturity would be like a trip on a freeway in an automobile which never had any mechanical difficulties, never ran out of gas or oil, never went off the road, and always maintained the same speed. Of course, development is not like that at all, either for the child or for the parent. The road is never straight or smooth, and the traveler sometimes swerves off the pavement. As one of our colleagues put it, after reading a draft of *Loving Your Children Better*: "I think I veered off on the farm to market road and now I can't find the highway." This chapter examines the roadblocks which adults sometimes unintentionally erect in the path of children's normal development.

As our experience with well-meaning parents has expanded, we have frequently asked ourselves and each other why parents have such a difficult time initiating and continuing consistent, systematic, thoughtful parenting plans. Even those who have managed children successfully usually cannot explain what they have done. Those parents who have had difficulties with their children have been equally puzzled. In the following discussion we draw upon our observations over the years in working with parents and their children.

Taking a Long Trip Without a Road Map:
Without a Well Thought-out Plan, Parents Are Forced to Parent Moment-by-Moment

Many parents do not really have a clear vision of the parenting process and how it works. This lack of clarity about what to do results in what we call "parenting moment-by-moment." In other words, parents devise a new tactic for handling each new behavior, whether acceptable or unacceptable, at the moment it occurs. The problem is aggravated by the notion that parenting is an intuitive process—we all know how to do it automatically. However, parenting moment-by-moment is an impossible task, given a child's vitality, enthusiasm and delightful curiosity. Such tactics result in frustration for parents and a failure to teach children that there are predictable consequences for both acceptable and unacceptable behavior.

Alternate Routes from Here to There:
Experts on Parenting Are Inconsistent

The number of books on the market about parenting is overwhelming. Concerned and thoughtful parents who have recognized their own parenting problems and sought to remedy an uncomfortable situation by reading works by experts probably come home from the bookstore with an armload of books offering contradictory advice. Having read many of these books ourselves, we have concluded that most contain useful, helpful and reassuring information. What is often unclear, and what makes for apparent inconsistencies among authors, is *when* to do what. A developmental approach, on the other hand, permits you to step back and see the "big picture" by providing the missing information about what to do, when to do it and why. One compelling example of this confusion is the issue of spanking. Some authorities suggest that spanking is a necessary, even vital, part of child-rearing while others contend that it should never occur in a loving home. From our perspective, spanking is an acceptable behavior management approach when the child is in a dangerous situation. When it is vital that your child remember that stepping into the street is prohibited, or that putting objects into wall outlets can be fatal, a pop on the fanny can be both necessary and effective. Recurrent spankings however, are not as effective as other behavior management techniques, and carry some disadvantages and negative long-term effects that other approaches do not.

How Far Along the Road Should My Child Be by This Time?

Parents Do Not Know What Is Developmentally Appropriate to Expect of Their Children

Well-meaning but uninformed parents who simply do not understand the limitations that development places on a child's abilities sometimes ask their children to do things that they are simply not able to do. This problem frequently arises as parents attempt to teach children manners. For instance, you may urge your toddler to share before he or she is able to understand the idea. Young children are not developmentally capable—that is, they do not possess the cognitive (or intellectual) ability—to share until age five or six. Sharing requires the capacity for seeing the world from another's point of view, a capacity which does not develop until that age. Younger children can only see the world from their own perspective. Preschoolers can be taught to give a piece of candy to a younger brother or sister, but only if they are praised and rewarded for doing so and not because they are sympathetic to the sibling's plight.

Toddlers can also be taught to say "please" and "thank you." Trouble usually crops up when parents cannot understand why their youngster does not spontaneously remember to use these phrases at the right times. Although most people do not recognize this, the appropriate use of "please" and "thank you" requires that the child be able to classify situations. Classification is a cognitive ability which gradually develops during early childhood, but is not present at birth. Teaching a child to say "thank you" to Grandma does not mean she will say "thank you" when she gets a sticker from her teacher at nursery school. A child cannot see these situations as belonging in the same category until she reaches five or six. Consequently, it is unreasonable to expect consistently polite responses to occur spontaneously until the child is school-aged.

Keeping Your Child from Getting Too Far Off the Road:

Parents are Afraid to Confront Their Children

Many parents seem reluctant to take a firm stand with their children. We have observed countless parents participating in exchanges such as this one: "You should not have hit Bobby. Hitting is not a nice thing to do. But you helped me pick up the house this morning, so today I won't punish you for hitting Bobby. Remember from now on, hitting is not nice." In this example, the child did not learn that hitting was unacceptable behavior. Hitting Bobby produced no negative consequences. In fact, what the child learned was that if he is helpful around the house, he can hit Bobby without having anything happen to him. We are quite certain that this is *not* what the parent wanted the child to learn!

We have also heard stories similar to the following. Mom discovers Julie playing with a ceramic unicorn and asks her to put it down. Julie does not comply, and later drops the unicorn, and breaks it. Mom hears the noise, returns to the scene, sends Julie outside, and sweeps up the broken pieces before Dad gets home from work. Julie has learned that she does not have to follow instructions from her mother, and that when she disobeys and breaks something, she gets to go outside and play.

We sometimes speculate about why parents are afraid to confront their children. Perhaps some parents do not realize that negative learning is occurring. Other parents may feel a strong need for their children to like them. Certainly, children function best in consistent environments where foreseeable consequences take place without undue outbursts of anger and consternation. In such situations, children can learn, misbehavior diminishes, and ultimately, children are happier. It has been said that the challenge of parenting is to turn your child into your friend, and we think parents can learn to do just that by providing a consistent, predictable environment during childhood.

Disagreements over Which Road Is Best:
Each Parent Has a Different Set of Rules

Too often one parent has one set of rules for the children and the other has another set entirely. These rules may involve anything from making beds in the morning before sitting down for breakfast to watching TV on school nights. Unfortunately, when specific behavioral consequences occur only with one parent, children are less likely to learn what is expected from them.

In addition, the disparity between parental responses to behavior often results in conflicts between the parents over how to handle the children. Sometimes these controversies escalate until more attention is paid to the other parent's "foolish ideas" than to the children's behavior. As the children grow older, they may learn to incite disagreement between parents—to "play off" one against the other—to get themselves out of a sticky situation.

Many parents easily sit down to talk about such family issues as the purchase of a new home or car, but not about what they want their children to learn or about how to handle a particular behavior. Houses and cars are of great concern, of course, but we encourage you to set aside time specifically devoted to careful consideration of your parenting strategies.

Detours Are to Be Expected:
Because Parents Do Not Understand Child Development, They Misinterpret Their Children's Behavior

As we have noted, many parents do not know *what* to expect from their children. The net result is that they do not understand what the child's behavior means and sometimes punish behavior for the wrong reason.

We recently heard a story told by the parents of five-year-old Jennie. Halloween was approaching, and this creative young child decided to concoct a "witch's brew" with some items from the kitchen, such as vinegar, ketchup and milk, and some from the bathroom, including Mom's expensive new perfume and Dad's favorite after shave lotion. Jennie mixed all the ingredients together and then divided her concoction into separate containers. Enraged, Jennie's parents spanked her, and sent her to her room without explanation. Had they understood that for children of this age, who are learning about concepts of size and volume, mixing and measuring are important parts of their intellectual development, the parents might have resolved the situation quite differently.

Jennie's parents could have provided some rather mild consequence for "using Mom and Dad's things without permission" and supplied her with a table on the patio complete with safe liquids and containers where she could mix to her heart's content. She might also be required to help clean up the mess in the kitchen. Because Jennie's parents did not realize the importance of this kind of play in the development of Jennie's cognitive abilities, they responded to a normal, understandable developmental behavior with an inappropriate punishment.

You Have to Steer More on a Bumpy Road:
Parents Are Consistent with Temperamentally "Easy" Children but Not with Temperamentally "Difficult" Children

Children's dispositions vary greatly. You will recall that children may be classified into three temperamental groups —"easy," "difficult," and "slow to warm up"— according to the central characteristics of their behavioral style. If you have ever compared your children to those of your friends, you have probably noticed that these stylistic differences manifest themselves soon after birth.

Parents, teachers and psychologists all find the "easy" children less trouble to manage. Parents seem to be more consistent with these children, and the children consequently become "easier" as the consistency builds their self-esteem and increases their adaptability. Not only are these kids generally quite happy, but their parents are also contented and confident of their parenting skills.

Parents of "difficult" children frequently feel stymied. The cycle which helped the "easy" children and their parents works in reverse for the "difficult" children and their parents. Even if the parents are consistent early in the child's life, the child's initial lack of responsiveness often breeds disappointment in parents. These overwhelming and confusing emotions can lead to inconsistency, which in turn increases the child's frustration and makes him or her more difficult. The more difficult the child becomes, the more frustrated the parents get, and the more they doubt their ability to parent. They often resort to physical punishment, even when they are philosophically opposed and feel uncomfortable with this approach. Parents of difficult children must realize that consistency and patience with these children will be rewarded in the long run. Should the situation get out of hand, some professional intervention may prove very helpful.

You Cannot Talk a Car Back onto the Road; You Have to Turn the Wheel or Step on the Brakes:
Parents Try to Manage Their Young Children with Explanations Rather Than Consequences

Many parents seem to be most comfortable when they explain to their children the reasons for the disciplinary technique they have chosen. As a result, these parents often do not identify the problem behavior and then manage it appropriately.

Most parents approach their children's behavior management using their own logical reasoning as a guide. Despite all good intentions, this tactic is doomed to failure for the most part because young children *cannot* reason logically. The developing brain does not mature enough to allow logical thought until about age 11.

The situation is far from uncommon; we have noticed that many middle-class parents attempt to reason with their kids. Negotiation and explanation, along with lots of patience, are the watchwords. As time passes, the parents' frustration increases, and the children's frustration increases. Parents are frustrated because reasoning alone does not work. Children are frustrated because they cannot understand. Ironically, by age 11, when their children can begin to understand logic and benefit from explanation and negotiation, most parents have given up these techniques.

One mother, herself a developmental psychologist, decided that she and her husband would explain to their son why they did what they did. Starting in Rob's infancy, each parental decision to put away a toy or stop the child from climbing on a piece of furniture brought forth a detailed explanation. By the age of three, Rob had developed some severe emotional problems. The psychiatrist whom the family saw for consultation told the parents: "In this age range, you have to be able to say 'no' and not always give a reason." As the mother underwent some soul-searching, she realized that as an adolescent she had desired to know the reasons for her parents' decisions—a desire which met with much frustration. Despite all her professional training, she had forgotten that a small child was simply not developmentally ready to process such information.

A common area of parent-child conflict involves homework. There is little to be gained from expounding upon why children must do their homework. Children must do their homework because the teacher assigned it, and because Mom and Dad said so. Explaining to children that completing their homework will ensure "getting a good job" or "making more money" years in the future is an exercise in futility. These events are too abstract and removed to motivate younger kids.

One eight-year-old boy referred for evaluation had developed great concerns about his grades. After numerous discussions with his well-intentioned father, he had arrived at the illogical and frightening conclusion that he would become a garbage man if he did not make straight

'A's. While it might be amusing to figure what his father had really said or meant, the result was that this boy reacted to getting 'B's on daily work with intense frustration and pain. It was later discovered that he had disturbing fantasies about "riding on a truck with all that trash."

Remembering the Roadblocks to Their Own Development:

Parents Generally Parent as They Wish They Had Been Managed During Their Adolescence

Parents' most typical memory of child rearing comes from their own last developmental stage. They recall their adolescent struggles and the management techniques instituted by their parents at that time. Even though it does not make much sense, most adults parent their own children in the way they would have liked to have been parented as adolescents. Typically, they conjure up as an ideal an understanding, gentle parent who would be suitable for an adolescent. Unfortunately, this approach does not work with toddlers. The kind of acceptance and understanding of an adolescent's tentative experimentation with alcohol or sexuality is neither appropriate nor helpful to a two-year-old whose fervent desire it is to extend bedtime until midnight or explore Dad's power tools.

People do carry into adulthood their psychological wounds from the teenage years. However, the parent who has given some long, hard thought to the parenting process and to the principles spelled out in this book should be able to differentiate between parenting approaches which are appropriate for very young children and those suited to adolescents.

While we certainly have not touched on all of the reasons for problems in parenting, we have tried to outline those we see most often. As a result of the mistakes described above, parents come to feel that parenting is a mysterious process with no predictable outcomes—a belief frequently leading to a feeling of helplessness that can contribute to further inconsistency. At worst, parents become distraught while children become distressed.

These distraught parents frequently reach irrational conclusions that only perpetuate their misery. They begin to think that their unruly offspring "just came that way" and yearn for children "like the Johnsons' kids" who seem so happy, responsive, and well-behaved. They decide that the key lies in "firm talking" or loud, angry disapproval for inappropriate behavior. Unfortunately, neither one is the key to mentally healthy, disciplined children.

It is informative to sit with these parents and watch a videotape of a well-behaved child. One can see the admiration and envy on their faces as they observe the child on tape willingly comply with such verbal requests as "Sit at the table," "Begin your work," "Fold the napkins," "Carry your plate to the kitchen now." When asked why the child behaved that way, some parents explain that she was responding to the "firmness in the parent's voice." When asked to try the same request with their own child, they try to imitate the tone and inflection of the voice on the tape. To their surprise, their child does not respond. They speak more loudly and more firmly, and still nothing happens. The parents are more certain than ever that something is wrong with their child.

We are convinced, however, that the child on the videotape has become responsive to verbal requests because she has a long history of management by behavioral consequences in the context of a warm, loving family environment. The child has learned to listen to her parents because in the past, failure to respond resulted in behavioral consequences for her. Simply stated, words alone carry sufficient authority when children have experience with the behavioral consequences which are associated with disregarding them.

For example, a child who consistently loses swimming privileges for failing to come out of the water at the first parental instruction, will eventually follow the family's "pool rules" without requiring consequences. What is more, through the process of generalization, this adherence to rules will spill over to other, unrelated areas. Once the desired pattern has been attained, parents have the luxury of managing their children solely with verbal admonishment and social disapproval.

In this chapter we have attempted to outline a variety of obstacles to normal development unwittingly erected by well-meaning parents. Recognition of these common problems often helps parents to clear the road for their children's happy and healthy developmental journey.

4

Looking Under the Hood: Developmental Building Blocks

Now that you have a general understanding of the developmental processes as well as some of the detours and roadblocks which may interfere with them, we are going to take a closer look at three distinctive elements involved in a child's growth: **feelings, thoughts** and **actions.** Just as when car maintenance is called for, you must determine whether you need to replace the fan belt, change the oil or add water to the battery, so parents must be able to distinguish among feelings, thoughts and actions, as each demands a different set of parental skills or responses. Confusing them—responding to the child's actions, for example, when you really need to deal with the child's feelings—can lead to ineffective parenting and frustration for parents and kids alike.

The specific guidelines that we will discuss in this chapter are summarized in the chart below.

Feelings	To understand your children, you must accept their feelings.
Thoughts	To respect your children, you must listen to their thoughts and ideas.
Actions	To manage your children, you must recognize their actions and establish developmentally appropriate rules of behavior.

In the following sections, we will show you how you may best recognize and handle feelings, thoughts and actions.

Feelings—The Building Blocks of Self-acceptance:

To Understand Your Children, You Must Accept Their Feelings

We cannot emphasize too strenuously the importance of investigating the nature of your child's feelings, whether the road is rocky or smooth. Internal reactions to events, feelings are reflected in changes in the physiological (body) state. For example, we have all experienced fear—the near-accident on the expressway, sudden turbulence in an airplane—and know that this emotion can result in increased heart and breathing rates as well as muscular tension.

Feelings become more complex as a child grows. Whereas a baby may only be able to experience polarities of joy and rage, these emotions eventually differentiate into a whole array from amusement to ecstasy and from irritation to extreme anger.

As most adults have probably learned from hard experience, it is impossible to talk someone—whether a grownup or a child—out of the way he or she "feels." Parents can aid their children in *coping* with their feelings, however, by following these suggestions.

Parent's Approach
(All Ages)

1. Encourage your child to identify feelings.
2. Encourage your child to verbalize feelings.
3. Accept your child's feelings without criticism.

Encourage Your Child to Identify Feelings

If you stop to think about it, you will realize that young children have little experience with their own feelings. Therefore, it is sometimes difficult for them to know just *what* they are feeling. Fortunately, adults can usually identify feelings for a child simply by observing the child's facial expressions and body language. Research into the psychology of body language has uncovered four basic feelings and facial expressions that seem to be universal: **sadness**, **anger**, **fear** and **surprise**.

Encourage Your Child to Verbalize Feelings

Parents can be immensely helpful to their child merely by encouraging him or her to put into words the emotions that they see their child experiencing. Both adults and kids find tremendous relief in being able to express feelings, especially those that are intense and troubling.

Learning to verbalize positive feelings is equally important, for such expressions are crucial to the establishment and maintenance of intimate relationships.

Encourage Your Child to Accept Feelings

Once a child's feelings have been identified and expressed, both parents and child need to accept those feelings in order to encourage the child's long-term emotional growth. In the short run, accepting the child's feelings may solve a problem that will eliminate the need for further action by the parent.

No matter what the feeling is, you must try to understand your child's emotions. We too frequently find parents telling a child, "You shouldn't feel that way." We suggest instead that the parent respond with something like, "I can see that you are angry (sad, frustrated, upset). Tell me about it...." Once the child has put the feelings into words, the parent may respond with a statement that is neither critical nor judgmental, but simply summarizes what the child has said. For example, "You are mad at Billy because he took your rubber stamp while you were still playing with it, and you wanted to hit him. You must have been awfully angry."

This approach is so powerful that parents who can listen and accept their children's expression of feelings frequently avoid having to initiate behavior management techniques to control their children's behavior. We recently heard a story about a gangly teenager who was facing a skills test in physical education class. Derrick stormed into the house after school demanding that his mother write a note excusing him from gym the next day. When she refused, he became angry and threatened to make her miserable for the rest of the week. Instead of responding in a confrontational way, Derrick's mother was able to listen and accept his anger about her refusal to excuse him; she encouraged him to talk to her about *why* he was so angry. As he talked, he became very sad and revealed how he was afraid that he would do badly on the push-ups and appear "wimpy" to the other kids. Once they talked about his feelings, Derrick calmed down and decided to do his best on the P.E. test. This mother's ability to listen and accept her child's feelings averted a major crisis.

Thoughts—The Building Blocks of Logic:
To Respect Your Children, You Must Listen to Their Thoughts and Ideas

Parents need to be aware of and concerned with their child's thinking as the child undergoes the developmental journey. Thoughts—mental, internal events which actually begin in infancy—cannot be observed directly, and are therefore not easily identifiable.

Many years ago, people believed that children reasoned in the same way as adults, only lacking the ability to hold and handle as much information. Intelligence was conceptualized as simply the child's progressive mastery of larger numbers of facts. Research into intellectual development has clearly and consistently disproven the notion of the child as a kind of "miniature adult." We now know that children's thinking evolves through identifiable stages. Children only gradually develop the capacity for logical thought as they grow older.

To borrow an image from the field of information processing: children are not small computers that increase their data base to form a large computer system; rather, their circuits become more complex as they grow and learn to plug effectively into the mainframe (society, or the collective body of knowledge). A child's intellectual development is more than the sum of its parts; that is, the changes a child undergoes in intellectual development are qualitative, as well as quantitative.

Parents must obviously tailor their approach to a child's intellectual development according to the child's current developmental stage. The following chart contains some general guidelines.

Child's Age	Parent's Approach
Until age 7	Listen and communicate that you care about your child's thinking. Logical arguments are not generally useful.
From age 7 to age 11	Analyze your child's thinking around knowable, concrete events. Logical arguments are occasionally helpful, but generally confuse the issue.

From age 11 through adulthood	Compare your child's thinking with your own and others' contrasting points of view. Evaluating logical strategies is important.

Until Age 7, Show Children You Care about Their Ideas by Listening

Prior to age two, thinking is confined to practicing sensory and motor schemes, such as exploring, touching, mouthing, grasping and kicking. Language development is elementary, and traditional signs of adult-like logic are absent.

Between the ages of two and seven, thinking shifts from an emphasis on sensorimotor skills to an emphasis on language skills and an understanding of simple classes (e.g., things that are round, things that are hot, things that are big). In this period, children conceive of the world in terms of extremes: love and hate, good and bad, big and little, pretty and ugly, nice and not nice. Later, their growing ability to integrate contradictory information will gradually allow them to like someone with whom they are angry, to see the good aspects of a bad situation, and so on. However, children between two and seven are extremist in their thinking, and parents should expect and accept such a style in their youngsters.

Until children reach the age of seven or so, parents should simply listen and communicate that they care about their child's thinking. Logical arguments are not useful, and parents cannot persuade their children to share their point of view. The consequences of trying to convince a four-year-old that he is being illogical usually prove quite unpleasant for both parents and child. His inability to think like an adult will result in the conversations degenerating into an argument, with both child and parents feeling angry, frustrated and misunderstood. Frequent repetitions of this situation will convince the child that his parents do not understand him. Parents of preschoolers usually leave these confrontations convinced that there is something wrong with their child, who is argumentative, stubborn or "impossible." Actually, parents can *create* argumentative children if they persist in these interactions which are biologically doomed to failure. Young children cannot reason like adults and are therefore, by virtue of their developmental level, "unreasonable."

During this early period, parents should concentrate on managing children's behavior (actions) through expectable consequences, and on understanding their children's feelings. Only when their children become biologically and psychologically *capable* of thinking like an adult, can parents talk to them on an adult level and expect an answer which is logical and reasonable (to the adult).

From Ages 7 to 11, Show Children You Care about Their Ideas by Analyzing Them Around Concrete Events

Between ages 7 and 11, children think in terms of concrete rules. Problem-solving is semi-logical, and often involves searching for a rule to apply to a situation. Consider the arithmetic tables which are generally mastered in this period; these are simply lists of rules about the relationships between numbers. You can understand your child's thinking if you limit yourself to concrete, expectable and knowable items and events. While logical arguments may occasionally be useful, they usually just confuse the child.

From Age 11, Show Children You Care about Their Ideas by Comparing Your Child's Ideas with Your Own and Others and Evaluating Logical Strategies

At approximately age 11 or 12, children's capacity for formal logic emerges. Just when many parents begin to wonder whether they speak the same language as their children, their eleven-year-old will say something so logical and profound that they cannot believe their ears. Such an occurrence heralds the need for parents to add a new set of skills to their repertoire.

Children's thoughts sometimes require change through confrontation and analysis. Confrontation does not mean angry demands for your child to alter how he or she thinks. Instead, confrontation means listening to your twelve-year-old daughter as she expresses her ideas, whether about the school cafeteria or a Supreme Court ruling, and gently raising the possibility that perhaps alternative or additional information might change her perception of how some part of the world works.

In this period, thoughts can be analyzed. The first analysis is triggered by the question, "Is that logical?" or "Is that rational?" or "Does that make sense?" Thoughts that cause problems for children often contain such words as "should", "have to", "always", "never" or "perfect"—words which imply extremes. This kind of thinking is left over from early childhood when thinking in extremes is the norm. At this later stage however, thinking in extremes can be challenged as illogical. Challenges to irrational thinking can lead to changes in the way children think. Thoughts can be changed, but only after children are old enough to think about their own thinking.

In summary, once their children reach age 11 or so and proceed into adolescence and adulthood, parents can compare their children's thinking with their own reasoning and that of others. Contrasting different points of view, raising various perspectives, and questioning the accuracy of various logical strategies, are all appropriate techniques.

Actions—The Building Blocks of Discipline:
To Manage Your Children, You Must Recognize Their Actions and Establish Developmentally Appropriate Rules of Behavior

The things that children *do* constitute the most visible aspect of the child's developmental journey. **Actions, which always involve moving some part of the body, can be described in simple, concrete terms: talking, running, smiling, hitting.** They can be stopped, started again, or replaced by the initiation of new actions. As actions are observable, your judgment of a child's behavior can be verified by others who watch the child. **Actions may stimulate reactions by parents: rewarding, ignoring or punishing.**

Early in your child's life, new actions or behaviors will emerge, primarily due to the process of physical maturation that is taking place. Tracking objects with their eyes, smiling, vocalizing, grasping and talking are just a handful of the actions that become possible for most children before they reach their second birthday. As children grow, the complexity of their actions increases. Peek-a-boo is supplanted by hide-and-go-seek, which may be replaced by elaborate fantasy games with other children, such as "Star Trek," which may in turn give way to backyard theatrical productions presented to the neighbors.

The cardinal feature of actions is that you can *see* them happen, and note them objectively, without interpretation or inference. In fact, when adults interpret an action or infer its meaning without permitting clarification by the child, mistaken conclusions may result. The teacher who reprimands a girl who laughs inappropriately is assuming that the child is fooling around, without recognizing that her laughter may be a sign of anxiety or embarrassment. Similarly, the parents of a boy who, hiding under his blanket and crying, at the last minute refuses to participate in a class play, may label his actions as "stage fright" when actually they reflect his reluctance to be seen in the green tights that his role demands he wear.

Not only can it be difficult for adults to determine what a given behavior really means, but often children do not understand it themsel-

ves. It is important that you look beneath the surface and question exactly what is causing the action—is there a particular unsettling or unpleasant feeling or thought which lies behind the undesirable or inappropriate action?

When parental intervention does become necessary, the parents' strategy depends largely on the child's developmental stage. While we will go into much more detail about our "Developmental Discipline" approach in Part Two of this book, we summarize the behavior management strategies available to parents in the following chart.

Developmental Stage	Parent's Approach
Infant Years (Birth to 2)	**Preferential Strategy:** Structure **Others:** Shaping, "No," Prompting, Ignoring, Positive Consequences, Negative Consequences
Toddler Years (Ages 2 to 4)	**Preferential Strategy:** Choices **Others:** Positive Consequences, Negative Consequences, Time-Out, Structure, Ignoring, Shaping, Prompting, Modeling
Early Childhood Years (Ages 4 to 7)	**Preferential Strategy:** Positive Consequences **Others:** Negative Consequences, Time-Out, Reward Charts, Choices, Modeling, Structure, Ignoring, Prompting, Shaping
School-Age Years (Ages 7 to 11)	**Preferential Strategy:** Social Agreements **Others:** Positive Consequences, Negative Consequences, Reward Charts, Choices, Time-Out, Modeling, Structure, Ignoring, Prompting, Shaping
Adolescent Years (Ages 11 to 18)	**Preferential Strategy:** Reasoning, Negotiation, Compromise **Others:** Positive Consequences, Social Agreements, Negative Consequences, Ignoring, Structure

Part Two

Introduction

If you stop and think about all the incredible changes that a child goes through—from complete dependency at birth to independence upon reaching adulthood—it is quite clear that to call the developmental journey "complex" is an understatement. We hope that this section will help eliminate some of the unnecessary complications by showing parents how to differentiate among and respond appropriately to their child's feelings, thoughts and actions.

Part One of this book has provided information about the "big picture" of the journey from birth to adulthood, a journey in which both the developing child and the loving parents participate. In a sense, reading Part One is much like looking at a globe: the major features—oceans and continents—are perfectly visible, and their relationship to each other is apparent, but it does not help much if you want to know how to go from New York to San Francisco. For that kind of specific information, one needs a road map with a little more detail.

Following Chapter 5's overview of the basic behavior management strategies, Chapters 6 through 10 deal with identifiable stages along the road to development. In Chapter 11, we look at the positive effects of the "Developmental Discipline" approach.

Remember, just as the best way to tell where you are along the highway is to look at the scenery and not at the clock, the best way to know how far along the developmental road children have gone is to watch what they do, to listen to what they say, and to analyze how they think, *not* merely to calculate how old they are. The ages with which we have delineated the five developmental stages from birth through adolescence are only approximations intended to be used as starting points, rather than hard-and-fast rules. In fact, we are certain that parents can learn to recognize developmental milestones so they will not have to rely on age to indicate which developmental tasks their child is facing.

We have divided Chapters 6 through 10 as follows:

Chapter 6	Infant Years (birth to two)
Chapter 7	Toddler Years (two to four)
Chapter 8	Early Childhood Years (four to seven)
Chapter 9	School-age Years (seven to eleven)
Chapter 10	Adolescent Years (eleven to eighteen)

Each of these chapters is set up in an identical pattern, starting with typical, recognizable and expectable occurrences for the period. The sections are listed below:

1. **Normal Development: Mile Markers**
   Here we describe the typical processes, developmental patterns and behaviors that characterize the period.
2. **Normal Development: Preventive Maintenance**
   This section outlines how parents can help facilitate healthy development in their children. As the heading suggests, such steps are as important to a child's development as checking the oil is to maintaining a car, and can prevent serious problems later on.
3. **Staying on the Road: Structure Is Best**
   Specific behavior management techniques, selected for their effectiveness and appropriateness to the developmental level, are described in this section. An asterisk appears beside the strategy of choice.
4. **Potholes in the Road: Do-it-yourself Tune-ups**
   Many behavior problems are "routine" in nature—i.e., irritating to the parents but not serious. This section discusses these typical problems and how parents may best handle them.
5. **Stopped on the Road: Call for Help**
   Finally, we list the signs of some of the more serious behavior problems which may require that parents seek professional advice.

Caution!

While the tendency may be for you to head directly to the behavior management sections of Chapters 6 through 10 to deal with a particular troubling situation with your child, we urge you to read the early sections in each chapter carefully. Before rushing to "solve" a problem by using a particular technique such as "negative consequences" or "time-out," ask yourself the following questions:

1. **Is the behavior of the child a normal developmental occurrence? That is, is it expectable in a given period?** If so, support it using the techniques outlined in the Preventive Maintenance section.
2. **Does the behavior of the child result from a temporary developmental regression? Has the child experienced an upset that causes him or her to act more immaturely than usual?** If so, again you should support the child using the techniques in the Preventive Maintenance section.
3. **Does the behavior result from an unidentified or unexpressed feeling?** If so, listen to the child, help the child identify and express the feeling, and communicate your understanding and acceptance.
4. **Does the behavior result from an unidentified or unexpressed thought?** If so, help the child identify and express the thought, and communicate your understanding and acceptance.
5. **Does the behavior require management?** If so, then turn to the appropriate section in the chapter which deals with children in your child's developmental stage.

5

Staying on the Road: Behavior Management Strategies

In this chapter we offer an overview of the behavior management strategies available to parents to help their children "stay on the road" in their journey to adulthood. Not every technique is appropriate to every developmental period. Nor is the same approach used precisely the same way from one stage to the next. In fact, it is crucial that these techniques *not* be viewed in isolation; rather, they must be put into the context of the developmental level of the child. To use the techniques indiscriminately would defeat the purpose of our book.

The following chart indicates the approximate ages at which particular techniques are most useful. The double asterisks (**) show the stage at which a technique is the preferred approach. For example, "positive consequences," useful throughout all stages of development, is the best technique in the early childhood years; at the other extreme, the "reasoning, negotiation and compromise" strategy, which is simply not viable before age 11 or so, becomes the most desirable method in the adolescent years.

Behavior Management Strategies for Each Period

	Infant Years Birth to 2	Toddler Years 2 to 4	Early Childhood 4 to 7	School-age Years 7 to 11	Adolescent Years 11 to 18
Structure	**	*	*	*	*
"No"	*				
Choices		**	*	*	
Positive Consequences	*	*	**	*	*
Reward Charts			*	*	
Negative Consequences	*	*	*	*	*
Time-Out		*	*	*	
Ignoring	*	*	*	*	*
Shaping	*	*	*	*	
Prompting	*	*	*	*	
Modeling		*	*	*	
Social Agreements				**	*
Reasoning, Compromise, Negotiation					**

*acceptable strategy
**preferred strategy

As you read the chapter which deals with your child's developmental level, you will find stage-appropriate examples to help you apply the suggested techniques. In addition, the preferred strategy for each period will be discussed in full in the designated chapter.

Here is an explanation of every technique presented in this book.

Structure

"Structure" is the term we use for changing the child's environment in order to:

- Prevent the occurrence of some undesirable behavior, and/or
- Facilitate the occurrence of some desirable behavior.

Structuring is useful throughout most of childhood, although the details will vary according to the child's level. For example, if you do not want your toddler to pull the dog's tail, you should simply put the dog outside. At the other extreme, parents who do not wish their adolescent to use the expensive, new car should make only the keys to the older car available.

In a more positive sense, structuring means providing opportunities for desirable behavior to occur. Parents can and should include objects or activities in the child's environment which are consistent with the child's developmental needs and the parents' values. For example, if parents want to foster a child's language development, they can buy the child records or tapes to play (or borrow them from the public library). Parents can help enhance large motor skills by providing a plastic bat and Nerf ball for use in the playroom or basement.

In our experience, parents often find it difficult to use structure consistently as a parenting technique, especially after the child develops some language ability. Rather, they are frequently tempted to try to reason with their children (an approach which, as we mentioned earlier, is unlikely to work prior to adolescence). Unfortunately, this also means that they are usually frustrated when their logical explanations fail to get their children to follow their instructions or to abide by their restrictions. Structuring the environment, as we have described it, offers parents a way of dealing with touchy situations without relying on the false hope that children will instantly respond to a verbal command. Rather, structuring makes undesirable behavior impossible.

"No"

Although parents who use structure advantageously will find the word "no" an infrequent part of their parenting vocabulary, every child will occasionally get into things that are either dangerous or somehow problem-causing. The simple and direct use of the word "no," recommended in the infant years only, can be an effective technique when accompanied by eye contact.

Choices

To utilize the "choices" technique, you simply offer the child two or three alternatives of things to do, all of which are okay with you. For example, a mother might tell her preschool-age son: "You can play cowboys and Indians outside or you can paint with watercolors inside." The child gets to decide what he wants to do, while the adult has structured the situation to include options that she can live with; now both can be happy. On the other hand, asking a child what she wants to drink when a soft drink is unacceptable or unavailable may be setting up both parent and child for conflict.

Positive Consequences

"If . . . then" conditions established by parents to get children to do something, "positive consequences" are usually stated by parents along these lines:

> "*If* you get dressed, *then* you may watch Sesame Street." [For toddlers]

Or,

> "*When* your list is all checked off (e.g., backpack organized, homework completed, clothes selected for the next day), *then* you may play Nintendo." [For older children]

In other words, a relationship or contingency is established between a child's **specific behavior** (desired by the parent) and a **particular consequence** (desired by the child). This technique probably sounds familiar to many readers because most effective parents and teachers use it.

The value of positive consequences as a management tool is directly related to parents' consistent willingness to follow through with the promised reward. Failure to follow through soon changes a positive consequence into an empty promise which will have little impact on a child's behavior.

We label consequences as either "logical" or "arbitrary" depending upon the nature of their relationship to the behavior within the situational context. Logical consequences, such as getting dessert if a child finishes her meal, follow from the specific behavior. Arbitrary consequences, such as a trip to the park if a child puts his clothes in the hamper, are not connected to the desired behavior. In some cases, logical consequences are too cumbersome or not effective or even realistically possible. At those times, parents can employ arbitrary consequences.

Please note that parents should only require behavior of children that they are capable of performing. To do otherwise would be totally contrary to the "Developmental Discipline" approach. Providing repeatedly inappropriate or impossible contingencies can prove harmful to normal development.

Reward Charts

"Reward charts" provide a concrete way of instituting positive consequences. Easily constructed in the school or at home, reward charts simply consist of a list of a few desirable behaviors and some means of monitoring these behaviors. For example, children may be given a check mark every time they hang up their coats, place their shoes on the door mat, help set the table, etc. These check marks are then exchanged for a sought-after activity or object, such as an outing at the zoo, or an inexpensive toy.

	SUN	MON	TUES	WED	THURS	FRI	SAT
Up when called							
Dressed by self							
Brush teeth							
Comb hair							
Make bed							
Give dog water							
Put p.j.s on							
In bed by 8:30							

For example, if 7 of the 8 items are checked per day, the child earns an agreed upon treat such as a sticker, prize or special activity.

As children grow older, the chart may become more complicated, with children earning weekly rewards as well as daily rewards.

Negative Consequences

Rather than promising to reward children for doing something you want them to do, the "negative consequences" strategy entails providing unpleasant consequences for some unacceptable behavior. As with positive consequences, this type of contingency depends upon the developmental level of the child. Negative consequences for toddlers should be brief and immediate. For teenagers, negative consequences, while potentially more stringent, should be negotiated. Examples include:

> "*If* you splash water onto the floor, *then* you will have to get out of the bathtub." [For younger children]

And,

> "*If* you use the car without permission, *then* you may not drive the car for a week." [For adolescents]

Negative consequences, then, involve taking something away from the child for misbehavior or for failing to do something the parent wants.

Negative consequences may be either logical or arbitrary. We should note here that some theoreticians (specifically, Dreikurs and Soltz) differentiate "natural" from "logical" consequences. They define natural consequences as those reflecting the nature of reality. For example, if a school-age youngster forgets his lunch box, he will be hungry at noon. According to this scheme, logical consequences are carefully designed by adults when natural consequences are not available. For example, the logical consequence of a child's refusing to take out the trash is her mother's refusing to cook in a kitchen permeated by an offensive smell. For our purposes, we have grouped these two notions together under the label of logical consequences—consequences which follow reasonably within the context of the situation. As discussed in the section on positive consequences, when logical consequences are either impractical or impossible, parents can utilize arbitrary ones.

The effectiveness of a negative consequence rests on the parents' ability to follow through with the response promised to the child. Each time a negative consequence situation is established and the promised outcome occurs, the more likely it becomes that the child will comply in the future. Conversely, each time the parent threatens some negative consequence and fails to follow through, the less likely it becomes that the children will pay any attention, since kids quickly learn to ignore an empty threat.

Another consideration is that **the consequence of the child's misbehavior has to be undesirable to the child.** For example, "If you leave your tricycle in the driveway, then it will be put away for the afternoon" will only work if the child is not already bored with the tricycle. If the presentation of this kind of contingency falls flat because the child does not care about the consequence, try another consequence or a different technique that carries with it an immediate impact.

While negative consequences can help effectively manage undesirable behavior, their potency decreases if used too frequently. We think that four of every five contingencies should be positive, and that parents who find themselves establishing negative consequence situations on a regular basis probably need to re-think their approach to parenting. Besides limiting the impact of the technique, utilizing negative consequences as a primary approach establishes a very unpleasant tone to parent-child interactions. Overuse of this technique usually means that parents have not considered how to set up positive consequences to reward more desirable behavior, or have not sufficiently structured the situation to prevent the undesirable behavior from occurring in the first place.

Time-out

"Time-out" is a specific negative consequence wherein the parent removes the child from doing some activity he or she likes and places the child for a specified length of time in a place where the activity is unavailable and there is an absence of stimulation. Usually that means that the child must sit for a short period in a chair or in a certain area, such as a hallway or a little-used guest room. Sometimes parents may elect to send the child to his or her bedroom. Parents do need to exercise caution when using the child's bedroom or the bathroom for time-out; it would be a mistake to have the child associate either of these rooms with unpleasantness.

In our clinical practices, we recommend that the length of the time-out should be relatively brief, with the number of minutes not exceeding the number of years in the child's age. In other words, a three-year-old would spend no more than three minutes in time-out, a five-year-old would spend no more than five minutes, etc. Although time-out is generally effective from the toddler years up to about age 10, we believe that the time-out period should not exceed seven minutes or so, even for the older kids.

Ignoring

Parents often underestimate the power of their attention (or lack of it) in managing children. Unfortunately, most of us are naturally inclined to pay attention to the annoying (and occasionally obnoxious) things which children do. Failing to notice a minor misbehavior—that is, *intentionally* failing to notice—usually will lead to the disappearance of that misbehavior. Although actively *not* noticing is difficult to learn, it is a powerful technique for eliminating undesirable behavior. **Ignoring is most powerful when combined with rewards for desirable behavior.**

Because this method results in relatively slow behavior change, it should not be utilized for actions that are highly aberrant or of serious concern to the family. However, for such unwanted behavior as a six-year-old's whining, a ten-year-old's complaints about the dinner vegetable, or an adolescent's outlandish clothing, ignoring is an appropriate strategy.

Understandably, sometimes parents become frustrated and cannot bring themselves to tolerate continued misbehavior until it fades away because of lack of attention paid to it. Parents say "I can't *not* notice" before ignoring has had a chance to work. For many parents, learning to count silently to twenty can be a good start.

Shaping

The process of rewarding any step, even a very small one, toward the goal you wish the child to achieve, "shaping" can be especially useful during the periods when children are learning to do many new things anyway because of their developmental stage. An example is children's experimentation with speech during infancy.

Parents will also want their child to learn to do things which are not developmentally motivated. Showing approval for a toddler's endeavors to dress himself or herself, even if the pants end up backwards, is an example of shaping. Gradually, parents can increase their expectations and raise the level of performance that is required to achieve reward. Thus, after the child has been consistently managing to get one leg in the pants, the parents can help the child get both legs in. Finally, they reward the child with a big smile and a "Good for you" after the child has managed to get both legs in the appropriate pants legs.

Shaping is also a good technique for dealing with older children in such behavioral matters as keeping their bedroom neat. This approach is gratifying because its effects can be seen readily, and because children naturally enjoy being praised for their efforts. The use of shaping also helps you resist the temptation to expect too much of your children or to punish them for their inability to meet unrealistic expectations.

Prompting

"Prompting" is one of the most frequently used methods for teaching young children new behaviors. It is a down-to-earth means of encouraging a child to do or say what the parent wants. Prompts may be either physical or verbal, with physical prompts (such as handing a child a toy to take into the bedroom) more appropriate in the early years, and verbal prompts more appropriate later in childhood.

The trick to effective verbal prompting is framing the reminder in a way that does not provoke an unnecessary power struggle. Rather than simply ordering a child, "Make your bed," the clever parent will ask,

"What are you supposed to do to your bed in the morning?" or casually remind the child, "Remember to make your bed before you go outside to play."

Modeling

Essentially a physical demonstration of a specific behavior, "modeling" offers parents another positive technique. For young children, parents will probably model behaviors involving table manners and simple, polite comments, such as "Thank you." When children are older, parents may make observations on specific social activities performed by others that they would like to instill in their child. For example, a father may remark on the mother's promptness in writing a thank-you note.

A milder technique than some of the others, modeling does have positive results, particularly if accompanied over time by verbal reinforcement (e.g., "You did a good job using your fork tonight") and other signs of approval.

Social Agreements

The "social agreements" approach is actually an adaptation of the previously discussed positive consequences method. Both strategies conform to the following paradigm: "*If* you do 'x,' *then* you may do 'y'" or "*When* you do 'a,' *then* 'b' will take place." What distinguishes social agreements from positive consequences is the *type* of reward provided by the parent. A consequence typically is behavioral and immediate in nature: "*As soon as* you get into pajamas, *then* you'll be able to have a bedtime snack." Social agreements, on the other hand, utilize interpersonal or social consequences: "*If* you take out the trash, *then* I'll play tennis with you this afternoon." Contingencies should shift from behavioral to social as the child grows older. Social agreements, which we introduce as the preferred strategy in the school-age years, are appropriate through adolescence.

There are three points to remember in using social agreements. First, **the consequences involve interpersonal activities either with the parent or peers.** Second, **the child *negotiates* with the parent on the desired consequences.** For example, it is not worth proposing a tennis game with your child if your child is uninterested in playing with you. Third, **the child can be at least partially responsible for arranging the subsequent reward.** A nine-year-old child can call a friend regarding a sleep-over; a thirteen-year-old can find out when bowling lanes are available.

Reasoning, Negotiation and Compromise

Because children's intellectual abilities develop gradually, the "reasoning, negotiation and compromise" approach is unlikely to meet with success before the adolescent years, when it becomes the preferred behavior management strategy. The emergence of logical reasoning skills in their teenagers allows parents to treat them as intellectual equals, at least to the extent that parents and teens possess the same cognitive powers.

Detailed examples involving two areas frequently marked by conflict, curfew and cars, are included in Chapter 10's discussion of this strategy.

It is our philosophy that when parents understand why their children are doing what they are doing and how children's behavior changes as the children grow, parents can follow up with logical and appropriate choices of responses. The parenting strategies we have described are enormously varied. We hope it is clear by now that we believe that there is no one "right" way of handling any situation with your child. For almost any behavior in every developmental phase there are always options—usually many of them—and parents must pick the ones with which they feel comfortable and which "match" the child's temperament and needs.

Remember that all children are different and each life journey unique. For this reason, development is enhanced when the trip is individualized for the particular child.

6

Infant Years: "Structure Phase"

Infant Years Chart

	Beginning:	Ending:
Approximate Ages:	Birth	2 years
Signposts:	Birth	Functional language and ability to imagine events that have not actually taken place
Normal Occurrences:	Attachment Basic trust Object constancy	
Primary Behavior Management Techniques:	* Structure Shaping "No" Prompting Ignoring Positive consequences Negative consequences	

By the "infant years," we mean the period extending from the birth of the child until the emergence of *functional language* and the *ability to imagine events* that have not actually occurred.

Despite its formal label, "functional language" simply refers to children's use of an object name and action word (that is, a verb) together in an appropriate way. Examples include "Daddy give" or "Baby go."

Children's ability to imagine events that have not actually occurred means that they can visualize an event without acting it out with concrete objects and/or physical movement. Throughout the infancy period, children lack the cognitive (or intellectual) capacity for imagining a situation in which they are not engaged. By the end of this stage, however, a child can visualize an action without actually doing it. For example, two-year-old Max can for the first time back up his tricycle before he opens the door so that the door will not bump into it.

The attainment of these milestones, usually around age two, marks the transition to the toddler stage. As we have emphasized, each child grows at his or her own pace, and it is the developmental phase rather than the age of a child that determines what parents should do to manage their children.

We have called this earliest period of development the "structure phase" because the primary recommended strategy for parenting is to *structure the situation* so that unwanted behavior cannot occur or desirable behavior is more likely to happen. We will delve into specifics later in this chapter.

Normal Development: Mile Markers

In this section, we explain the developmental processes and patterns typical of the infant years, focusing on the areas of **attachment, basic trust** and **object constancy.** Because these are normal occurrences, we urge parents to tolerate any difficult behaviors associated with them and avoid punishment. If you struggle with your child over these issues, conflicts may persist well beyond this stage. On the other hand, patience and understanding will help your child progress smoothly over any expectable bumps along the way.

Attachment: Bonding to a Primary Caregiver

The first and probably most important developmental task for any child is the formation of an attachment between child and parent or primary caregiver, usually the mother. Research has repeatedly confirmed the centrality of the emotional interaction between mother and child to the child's psychological and physical well-being. In fact, the mother-child attachment seems to be so vital that a child can die if deprived of this loving relationship.

Developmental psychologists' interest in attachment was heightened after several classic studies found that infants who were separated from their mothers during their first year of life became listless and unresponsive to their environment, and displayed less motor activity. Strikingly, the children's suffering occurred despite the fact that their physical needs were more than adequately cared for by conscientious, dedicated professionals who maintained very high health standards.

Just taking care of your child's physical needs is not enough. **Physical touch, emotional attention, prompt response to cries,** and **loving interactions** are all essential.

Attachment occurs in a predictable developmental sequence. Especially at first, the quality of children's attachment is limited by their physical development. At birth, and for a few months afterward, children just cannot see as well as adults. Their hearing is also less well-developed than that of adults. In addition, their tiny brains are still growing connections. Until those connections between neurons are made, children's ability to interpret and understand what they see or hear remains limited. Consequently, infants have a somewhat restricted capacity for discriminating between different sights and sounds as well as a limited means of interacting with the world. As all parents soon discover, infants do react to gross changes in their environment: when they feel good (warm, dry or well-fed), they coo contentedly; when they feel bad (cold, wet, hungry or uncomfortable), they cry or fuss.

Later signs of attachment, made possible by the growing child's increased ability to discern differences among stimuli (sights and sounds), appear when the child shows some preference for the familiar. If a child has received care primarily from a female figure, he or she will now display a preference for female voices. Later, the child will favor the caregiver's voice, specifically. Children also prefer familiar sights during this period, and frequently shy away from new ones. Although it may prove disconcerting to Mom, it is not unusual for a child to fail to recognize her when she puts on her glasses or tries a different hairstyle, as this face is different from the remembered face.

"Stranger anxiety" usually emerges around seven months. This new phenomenon signals that children now have an elementary recognition of familiar stimuli since they react to unfamiliar stimuli with alarm. Uninformed parents are sometimes needlessly embarrassed by their children's behavior during this phase. Mothers and fathers can experience dismay when their eight-month-old baby cries with fright when guests or grandparents have come to visit. They may be puzzled about the difference between the baby's model behavior during these same people's last visit a few months ago, and the strong reaction they see now. The tears and fright reflect the child's increasing ability to distinguish strangers, as well as a developmentally expectable difficulty in adjusting to an overload of new stimuli. Contradictory as it may seem at first, stranger anxiety is a sign of continuing normal development.

Other typical behavior during this period includes more frequent vocalizing for the primary caregiver, heightened distress during her absence, and generally increased crying. Parents sometimes seek consultation with pediatricians or child psychologists when the infant reacts so strongly to events that seem minor to the parents. There is usually no cause for alarm, however, as the intensity of the reactions will diminish as the child develops. Once parents are taught to notice the connection between the mother's absence and the child's real distress, their fears are generally laid to rest.

We might point out that stranger anxiety typically reappears during the second year of life, most often between 15 and 18 months, when the child is sensitive to separations from and reunions with the mother or primary caregiver. Therefore parents should not be surprised when some of the earlier behavior repeats itself. This seemingly immature behavior will persist through the conclusion of infancy and well into the toddler phase, ending around the age of three.

Basic Trust: Learning to Rely on Others

During the period from birth to two years, children develop a sense of basic trust or mistrust that is the bedrock for later psychological growth. Many parents erroneously believe that children make this choice based on the quality or quantity of their feedings. While it is true that the parents' immediate responsiveness to the child's cries for food is one contributing factor, basic trust really depends on the parents' ability to provide a safe, predictable, comfortable environment for their children. That means being responsive to all their needs during this period: responding to them when they cry, feeding them when they are hungry, changing them when they are wet, and helping them fall asleep when they are tired. It also means talking to babies—providing them with information about the objects and people in their world as they begin to try to understand and master it—and playing with them. **Ignore dire warnings from well-meaning but misinformed friends or relatives: children cannot be "spoiled" during the first year of life.** To the contrary, leaving an infant to cry for extended periods of time is detrimental and results in insecurities and a lack of trust later in life.

Object Constancy: Developing the Ability to Hold onto Mental Images

The most important intellectual milestone in the first two years of life is the development of "object concept," an internal memory of a real, recognizable, specific external object or person. Babies first come to recognize and remember very familiar adults and physical objects, such as bottles, rattles, and toys. They recognize and remember unfamiliar people a bit later. Some "object constancy"—that is, the ability to maintain a mental image—is already established by the first year. By the time children approach their second birthday, they are well on their way to having stable object concepts for many people.

Careful study of very young children has identified specific subphases of this early developmental period. The subphases are based on the development of infants' sensory and motor systems. As these systems advance, children are better able to explore and subsequently recognize objects and people.

During the first subphase, which lasts from birth to about one month, the child's sensory and physiological systems are still largely undeveloped. In other words, newborns have little recognition of the world around them.

The second subphase begins around one month and ends around four months. Infants now follow an object with their eyes. They may search for their bottle if they can see the nipple, but not if the nipple is out of sight. At this early stage, babies recognize certain aspects of objects, although probably not the object as a whole.

The third subphase extends from approximately four months to eight months. Children now can manipulate physical objects, and they will search for one which is partially hidden if they can see a portion of it—for instance, even the non-nipple (that is, the non-central) part of the bottle. Intriguing actions will be repeated. For example, when infants bump into a mobile in their crib and it jiggles, they will try to hit it again.

Beginning at eight months or so, when infants are first shown an object which is then completely hidden from them, they will actively search for it. They have become very interested in the physical world around them by this time, and are likely to explore objects from every angle. Examining a stuffed animal, Mom's purse, a fringed throw pillow or any other object from all sides, an infant will turn it over and over, feeling every contour and crevice. This phase, so enchanting for parents to observe, ends as the first birthday nears.

Between 12 and 18 months, children will begin to search for objects where they last saw them. This activity signifies the continuing consolidation of internal object concepts, since one must be able to recognize and remember an object to search for it in an organized fashion.

By the time children reach the final subphase, which lasts from 18 months until age two, they have developed considerable capacity for recognizing both objects and people. Moreover, they can contemplate an action without having to perform it, as they did during the earlier periods. For example, a child will now be able to figure out that she must turn a large toy sideways to get it into a playhouse; earlier, she would have tried pulling it through unsuccessfully before figuring out that it does not fit that way. This new ability marks a milestone in children's cognitive development: for the first time in their young lives, thinking and acting are independent processes.

Normal Development: Preventive Maintenance

Parents are often concerned about what they can do to help their children in the development of the natural psychological processes which we have just described. This section contains a list of methods parents can adopt to contribute to the creation of **attachment, basic trust** and **object constancy** in their children.

Techniques to Build Attachment

The most powerful way to build attachment is to be responsive to the child's physical and emotional needs. Good caretaking means feeding children as soon as they are hungry, changing their diapers when they are wet, and soothing them when they are upset. Good caretaking also means responding to children's emotional needs. Infants need to be cuddled, hugged, talked to, played with and loved. Remember, before one year of age, a child cannot be "spoiled," only neglected.

As you will recall from the section on temperament in Chapter 2, children vary in their preference for physical contact. Temperamentally difficult children may actually prefer less contact and lower levels of stimulation. If you observe your child carefully, you should be able to determine how much holding and cuddling is pleasing to him or her. Your child's behavior should serve as the ultimate guide.

Sometimes circumstances make it difficult to provide generally positive experiences for a child during this period. Some mothers are so anxious about parenting that they find it hard to relax around their babies. Children can sense this nervousness, and they themselves may become tense, and therefore more unhappy and difficult to care for. The mothers then become even more anxious about their ability to be good mothers, and the cycle of maternal anxiety and child distress continues to escalate. Anxious or angry mothers may need short-term counseling to give them the confidence they need to interact calmly with their children.

The following practical suggestions for facilitating attachment are aimed at mothers, fathers and primary caregivers:

1. **Be consistently available to your child.**
2. **Go to your child when your child needs you.** Take care of your child's physical and emotional requirements.
3. **Take time for yourself and engage in satisfying interactions with other adults or children.** Pursuing outside interests will increase your ability to provide consistently loving, responsive care for your baby.
4. **Anticipate the "one step forward, two steps backward" nature of development in your child.** Recognizing progression and regression as normal parts of the developmental process will allow you to cope better with your child's repeated gains and losses of new skills.
5. **Love your child.** Enjoy being close to your baby.

Techniques to Build the Development of Basic Trust

Parents can take these simple steps to help their babies develop a sense of basic trust:

1. **Strive for regularity in feeding, sleeping and bathing.** Maintain the same sequence of activities when possible. For example, the baby may wake up, eat and then take a bath.

2. **On the other hand, do not be rigidly bound to a schedule.** Allow yourself flexibility in responding to the child's apparent needs.
3. **Talk to your infant while you take care of him or her.** Maintain eye contact as you tell your child what you are doing.
4. **Play with your child several times every day.**
5. **Enjoy your baby.**
6. **Plan carefully for transitions, such as beginning child care at a sitter's home.** Give your infant opportunities to become familiar with new situations or people. For example, you may want the child to meet the new sitter two or three times before you actually leave the child with her.
7. **You may minimize the trauma of separation for your baby by providing him or her with special objects.** A favorite toy or an article of your clothing may help soothe a very young baby when you are absent. In later infancy, a concrete reminder such as a photograph may serve the same purpose.
8. **You must tell your babies that you are leaving.** Since some children will protest, there is no need to tell them far ahead of time. A quick "bye-bye" hug and kiss seem appropriate.

Techniques to Build Object Constancy

Parents can facilitate the development of object constancy in the following ways:

1. **Provide your infant with lots of sensory experiences in all sensory modes: auditory, visual, tactile (touch) and kinesthetic (bodily movement).** These experiences might include singing, listening to music, watching mobiles, exploring interesting textures, swinging and hugging. Do realize, however, that you can overstimulate a baby at times. Should the baby cue you by crying, do give him or her a rest.
2. **Encourage play and exploration with toys and people.**
3. **Encourage naming and recognition of toys and people.**
4. **Play hide-and-go-seek and peek-a-boo with your child.** As the youngster's ability to search expands, gradually increase the difficulty of the game.
5. **Encourage imitation of your voice and your gestures, and imitate your baby's voice and gestures.**

6. **Provide developmentally appropriate toys.** Remember the developmental pattern and fit the toys to the stage. Many household objects are appropriate.

Developmental Ability:	Appropriate Toys:
Grasping	Rattles, rings, plastic keys
Mouthing	Safe objects to chew on
Visual inspection	Anything visually stimulating; bright colors (particularly red), interesting, dramatic patterns and shapes (particularly black and white), nonbreakable crib mirrors
Hitting	Toys on suction cups attached to furniture
Dropping and throwing	Small balls, bean bags, unbreakable objects
Showing	Any safe object
Giving	Any safe object
Naming	Any safe object
Use in symbolic play	Any safe object

CAUTION

Staying on the Road: Structure is Best

This section contains the management techniques, or parenting strategies, which we have found to be the most successful with children in the infancy stage: **structure, shaping, "No," prompting, ignoring, positive consequences** and **negative consequences.** These approaches work because they are well-matched to the developmental needs of children from birth to two years, and to the goals of parents who want to help their children grow during this period.

For more complete definitions and an overview of behavior management techniques, we refer the reader to Chapter 5.

* *Structure*

"Structure" is the technique that makes changes in the environment so that:

1. Children can do what parents want them to do, and
2. Children cannot do what parents do not want them to do.

It usually begins with parents keeping dangerous objects and substances out of reach of young children, who typically put any new object in their mouth first. When babies start getting around by rolling or crawling, parents must "child proof" their home, placing safety guards in electrical outlets, removing reachable extension cords, and so on. After babies are walking, structuring means locking lower cabinets containing cleaning supplies, moving potentially dangerous or breakable objects up out of reach, securing doors to rooms that contain such objects, and fastening gates guarding stairs.

Structuring really involves commonsense decisions. For example:

- If you do not want your child to fiddle with the computer equipment and open the desk drawers in your home office, keep the door locked.
- If you do not want your child to play with his or her genitals in public, dress your child in overalls.
- If you do not want your child to break the glass vase you received as a wedding gift, put it up until your child is older.

Consider the alternative. You can camp out in the living room next to the coffee table and say "No!" every time your child looks at the vase. How exasperating for both child and parent. Structuring reduces the number of unpleasant interactions that parents are forced to have with their children.

Of course, structuring also means providing the opportunities for your children to do what you want them to do. For very young babies, that might mean putting a mobile in their crib to encourage the development of visual-motor skills. For two-year-olds, it could mean supplying Nerf balls to kick or throw, a back yard sandbox to play in, and a quiet time with you to talk or cuddle or take a walk.

In dealing with children at this stage, structuring the situation is the most effective way to control the child—to say nothing of minimizing parents' frustration. Take a look around the room or the house where your child will be. If you see an object which is "off-limits"—that is, when your child touches it, the action will elicit a "No!" from you—simply remove it. If there are more than a couple of those "no" objects around which you cannot place out of reach or remove altogether, consider putting the child somewhere else, for your sake and your child's.

Many parents use playpens to keep their children out of danger or mischief. While we feel this may be okay on an occasional basis, we do not recommend that parents place children in playpens very often, as infants need to explore their environment for optimal development.

Shaping

During the first two years, children achieve remarkable progress in acquiring control over their bodies. From being unable to make any controlled movement at birth, by age two children will have progressed to walking, running, talking and playing. At each step along the way, parents can use the "shaping" technique by encouraging their child in any effort to reach the next developmental level. For example, parents can smile and pat the baby who first tries to roll over for any attempt to do so, no matter how successful, should be encouraged.

Eating is one area where shaping can prove particularly helpful. At first, the child will be rewarded for any movement of the spoon toward her mouth: "Spoon up. Good job!" The next spoonful that gets still closer will also elicit praise: "That's great, you almost made it to your mouth!" Finally, when spoon and mouth collide: "That's terrific, you got the food all the way to your mouth!"

In a similar way, parents can encourage children's use of a cup. At first they will offer the child a very small amount of juice in a cup with a lid and drinking spout. Over time, as the child develops skill with the special cup, more juice can be added. Eventually the child will be able to drink successfully from a cup without any lid at all. At each point in this long and sometimes messy process, lots of praise is in order.

"No"

A firm "No" while looking the child in the eye is a useful management technique, even for very young children who do not have language tools. Establishing eye contact is important, as research has demonstrated that looking children in the eye makes it four times more likely that they will comply with the instruction.

Do note that the effectiveness of this technique is limited by the frequency with which it is used. The more often "No" is used, the less effective it becomes. As mentioned above, structuring the environment is probably the best way to reduce the number of times you must tell your child "No."

Examples of situations which may call for child's opening and rummaging in a neighbor's kitchen drawer, approaching a strange dog while on a walk, or poking at a stack of cans at the supermarket.

Prompting

"Prompting" encourages children to behave in the way that parents desire. At this stage in children's development, physical prompts are more effective than verbal ones. For example, a parent will put an arm out to prevent a child from walking into the street, or sit beside a child on the floor to help pick up blocks and put them away.

Parents do need to help children accomplish many tasks during this phase. Prompting may help to initiate the action, but because of children's immaturity, they cannot complete most tasks independently.

Ignoring

Withholding attention from an undesirable behavior can lead to the gradual extinguishing of that behavior. For example, in the later stages of infancy "ignoring" works well in the all too frequent experience of a child's screeching. Rather than scolding or spanking, the parents simply continue their current activity. When the child starts speaking softly again, the parents can acknowledge the change with a simple verbal expression of pleasure.

Ignoring is most effective when there are no other adults or children around to provide the attention you are so carefully withholding.

Positive Consequences

"Positive consequences" promise a child that when he or she has performed a specified behavior, the parent will do or allow something that the child wants. Such statements follow this format: "*If* you hand me the toy, *then* you may have a grape."

As youngsters approach 18 months or so, parents can begin introducing these verbal conditions to familiarize children with the notion of consequences. Because of children's cognitive and physical limitations, parents will need to help children perform as desired by "walking them through" the task. Inclusion of positive consequences as a behavior management strategy in this period of development is intended *only* to familiarize children with the process; it is certainly not a primary strategy. Parents are cautioned against using this technique too often during the infant years.

Negative Consequences

This technique, which involves parents warning children about the outcome for some undesirable behavior, should not be used before children are 18 months or so and their mobility gets them into trouble. If parents are applying structure correctly, then "negative consequences" need only be utilized in situations which are dangerous and/or unpredictable. Remember that negative consequences should only be used infrequently and for the purpose of familiarizing young children with the idea of consequences.

Here are two pertinent examples. If a child runs into the street, the parent might give him a pop on the fanny. Or, if a child swings a heavy bat toward her brother, the parent can restrain her while counting to ten. Whatever the situation, the consequences should be immediate and brief. Measures such as forcing a child to sit on a chair for five minutes are simply inappropriate at this stage.

Parents are cautioned to tread lightly in the area of negative consequences when dealing with a one- to two-year-old. Sophisticated use of this approach will have to wait until the child reaches a later developmental stage. As with positive consequences, at best a parent can only introduce a child to the concept.

Potholes in the Road: Do-it-yourself Tune-ups

In this section we discuss some of the "routine behavior problems" which crop up during the infant years and suggest ways in which parents may handle them. These problems include **dangerous or frustrating situations, sleep difficulties,** and **children's reactions to frightening situations.**

Dangerous or Frustrating Situations

Parents soon find out how alert they must be in dealing with their infants, especially as they grow older. As children's mobility increases, their ability to provoke dangerous circumstances increases as well. However, even as children's curiosity expands, they still lack the intellectual skills to tell the difference between what is dangerous and what is not. Parents frequently complain that their young children play with unsafe objects (electrical outlets, hot stoves, household chemicals), provoke pets and older children, and cause household accidents (by pulling a lamp from a table or pushing objects over, for instance).

The best strategy for managing these problems is to employ the technique which we have called "structure." As you will recall, structuring is accomplished by either changing the environment or removing the child. Changing the environment can be done in any of a thousand ways.

- If you do not want your daughter to put her fingers in the electrical outlets, purchase inexpensive, child-proof plastic covers for them.
- If you fear that your son will get into the housecleaning chemicals, lock them away safely.
- If your child constantly provokes the family pet, separate them.

Sometimes structuring the environment means making decisions that affect the entire household or may even disappoint one or both parents. For instance, no matter how much fun you feel a pet would be for parents and child, if you do not already have a cat or dog we recommend that you put off getting one until the child is older. Infants cannot yet control their own behavior sufficiently well to interact responsibly with an animal.

Unfortunately, parents frequently fail to manage the environment and attempt to lay down rules which they cannot possibly enforce and which the child is just too young to follow. As a result, parents spend too much of their time saying "No" and running to catch the vase before it hits the floor! Much disappointment and frustration can be avoided by structuring the environment so that unwanted behavior cannot occur.

When the environment cannot be changed satisfactorily, the child must be removed from the dangerous or problem-causing situation. For example, this may be necessary when parents visit in homes where they cannot cover the outlets or remove the expensive furniture. Parents are sometimes exasperated when their children cannot be controlled in these situations, and therefore do not enjoy their visits. Many times the best strategy is to arrange to leave an infant at home or with a familiar friend or relative while the parents go on a visit.

At times parents may become so fatigued with keeping their child safe and out of trouble that they find themselves disliking the child. Parents should be assured that these feelings are normal. However, if these feelings are allowed to build, they can lead to real problems in the parent-child relationship. A negative cycle may start in which the emphasis placed on negative interaction can ultimately short-circuit the loving interaction between parent and child. If such a cycle seems to have begun, structure techniques should be instituted immediately to restore a positive relationship between parent and child.

Sleep Difficulties

Children vary enormously in how much sleep they require. For example, some newborns will sleep almost continuously in the first week, while others may never sleep more than 10 to 12 hours per day. This variability between children persists throughout the infancy period and childhood. Incredible as it may sound to bleary-eyed parents, children in this period rarely have sleep problems unless they are ill or mistreated. They will sleep when they need to as long as they are fed and comforted. The problem, of course, is that children's sleep patterns do not always correspond with parents' needs or wishes.

Babies awaken because they finish sleeping. Generally it is not possible to put a baby back to sleep. This is a situation that parents simply have to deal with, and cannot change. **If you try to force a baby to sleep when he or she is not ready, the child may in fact develop real sleep problems.**

It is not uncommon for children to have some trouble getting to sleep from time to time during this period, particularly in response to new situations or changes in routine. While parents often find it hard to be consistent, the time and effort spent establishing a systematic bedtime routine is well worth it. The nighttime ritual should include a specific series of events, such as taking a bath, putting on pajamas, drinking milk, hearing a bedtime story, cuddling with a favorite stuffed animal, drinking water (which also protects against tooth decay) and kissing goodnight. While the specifics will differ from family to family, the important thing is that the same actions are done in the same order night after night. Children are reassured by such rituals, and will even become distressed if the series is not precisely followed. Remember that parents need to institute these rituals when children are ready to sleep, not when parents want them to sleep.

Parents may also encourage a child to sleep by sitting or rocking with the child for a short time until he or she is sleepy. Parents should be cautioned about stimulating children by talking to or playing with them, however, while preparing them for sleep.

Often children won't go to sleep without displaying some signs of dissatisfaction with the situation. Some authors of books on baby care argue that you should leave your child to cry no matter how long it takes the child to fall asleep; others say not to leave or let the baby cry at all.

Until a child is about one year of age, we recommend techniques that head off tears and upset. Parents should make every effort to soothe their baby and make bedtime as pleasant as possible. Once a child is about a year old, we recommend a middle ground between leaving the child desperately alone and allowing the child success in getting up again and again. The parent should return every five minutes or so for as long as the child fusses, but stay only long enough to tuck the child in, smile, say goodnight and leave again.

Children's Reactions to Frightening Situations

During this early developmental period, children are easily and frequently startled and even frightened when exposed to new people, places and things. Parents sometimes forget that young children are seeing an object or place for the *first* time, even though the parents may have literally seen it hundreds of times. No one can blame children for being anxious about things they have never seen before and do not understand. Armed with this knowledge and the expectation that their children may react negatively to new situations, parents should be better equipped to help their youngsters to adjust by anticipating anxiety-provoking situations and thereby limiting children's exposure to them when possible. Being ready to comfort and reassure your child is also important.

Once again, the preferred strategy is to structure the situation to suit the child. **We recommend that parents introduce young children to any new place, object or occurrence gradually, slowly increasing their exposure to new situations until they are no longer afraid.** Throwing babies in the air, taking them into the shower, or letting them ride a carousel are just three examples of situations parents think should be fun but children may react to with fear.

One of us recently watched as a young child confronted his very first dog. Joey's mother was visiting a family friend, whose extremely friendly Collie came bounding into the house where the boy was toddling about. The dog jumped up in his excitement, and put a paw on the child's chest. When Joey reacted with terror and began to cry, the dog was taken outside. The mother held Joey and told him, "Dog jumps," while Joey watched through the window as the dog jumped. After repeating "Doggie jumps" several times, he calmed down. This is an excellent example of how gradual re-exposure (watching the jumping dog through the window) and simple information matched to the child's level of cognitive development can seemingly work miracles.

For Joey, actually touching the dog might eventually be the appropriate next step. Of course, every child reacts differently to new situations, and parental responsiveness to a child's fears is extremely important. **Parents need to remember that exposure is based on when the child is ready, not when the parents want the child to be ready.**

As the section on attachment indicated, there are two periods when children are usually afraid of new people. The initial period occurs as the child first develops the ability to distinguish faces, at about six to eight months. The second normal period of stranger anxiety occurs at about 15 to 18 months, and is caused by the child's growing sensitivity to separations from the mother. These situations do not need management, just understanding and parental recognition that they will pass as the child develops. This means parents should comfort the child as needed and not force the child into situations with new people that frighten him or her. Let the child's reactions guide you.

Children are vulnerable to the development of fears and phobias during this developmental period because of their limited cognitive abilities. As they cannot distinguish imagination from reality, monsters, ghosts and bogeymen are real to very young children, and no amount of logical discussion will convince them that they do not exist. These fears, which sometimes persist until children are four or five years old, usually fade away as children's cognitive skills enable them to distinguish reality from fantasy.

Stopped on the Road: Call for Help

The vast majority of children develop no serious difficulties during this phase, and parents can simply enjoy their babies. About one baby in a thousand, however, will incur some problem necessitating professional evaluation or intervention. This section lists the kinds of behaviors which serve as red flags warning parents to seek professional help for their child: **failure to thrive, failure to attach**, and **developmental delays.**

In general, we feel that parents often benefit from consultation. Professionals can provide information regarding developmental norms that may put parents minds at rest. They can make suggestions as to how to handle difficult situations. In addition, parents' anxiety may be alleviated by talking with professionals about their feelings regarding childrearing. **If you have any concerns about your child or about your skills as a parent, we encourage you to seek outside help.**

Failure to Thrive

Some babies just do not seem to gain weight or to grow more alert and active during their first year. Infants who remain listless, small for their age, and inattentive into their sixth month need to be evaluated by the pediatrician, who may then make referrals to other professionals.

Failure to Attach

Sometimes babies develop normally physically, but do not seem very interested in people. Social smiling does not occur or occurs very late. These babies may express interest in objects, however; mobiles or wheels may excite them more than members of the family. By the end of the first year, these babies are noticeably unresponsive to people when compared to other babies, and seem preoccupied with their own internal world. They also are slow to acquire understanding of language, and even slower to develop the ability to talk. These trends become more obvious as time passes, and do not fade out in the way that they do in normal children. Parents who detect failure to attach in their infants should take them for evaluation by the pediatrician, who may call upon other specialists for consultation.

Developmental Delays

Children can sometimes be delayed in the development of large or small motor skills, sensory abilities, cognitive skills or language. Although in most cases delays are not meaningful, sometimes they may indicate problems which warrant further evaluation.

When parents do not know the developmental norms, it can prove very upsetting. We heard the story of one concerned mother who worried because nine-month-old Janie was not keeping pace with the already walking nine-month-old Melissa down the street. The more she kept comparing Janie with Melissa, the more she worried. When she approached the pediatrician, the latter assured her: "There's nothing wrong with Janie—she's right on schedule. It's that girl down the street!" Because this mother mistook Melissa's acceleration for the norm, she misread her own daughter's development as a "delay."

Parental errors can be made in the opposite direction as well. Bradley, who was the child of older parents living in a neighborhood where there were no other babies, had not begun to walk by 19 months of age. Because his parents were unfamiliar with the norms, they did not question Bradley's development. His pediatrician picked up on the situation at the boy's two-year check-up and made a referral to a specialist to determine the nature and extent of the delay.

Clearly, parents cannot know the norms in every area of development. If parents have concerns, they should visit their pediatrician to determine whether there is indeed a delay, and whether it warrants further evaluation.

7

Toddler Years: "Choices Phase"

Toddler Years Chart

	Beginning:	Ending:
Approximate Ages:	2 Years	4 Years
Signposts:	Ability to imagine events that have not actually occurred and emergence of functional language	Start of cooperative play
Normal Occurrences:	Autonomy Separation/Individuation Self-control Symbolic thinking Self-centered point of view Over-reliance on perception Conformity to avoid punishment	
Primary Behavior Management Techniques: *	Choices Positive consequences Negative consequences Time-out Structure Ignoring Shaping Prompting Modeling	

Generally speaking, the toddler years last from about age two until four, although some experts consider the period to range from one and a half to three years.

The beginning of this period is characterized by the child's *ability to imagine events* that have not actually occurred and the emergence of *functional language* (sentences with a subject and verb which communicate a complete thought). The phase ends with the start of *cooperative play;* children now talk to each other about the same subject and interact in a meaningful way.

During the toddler years, children's play is actually parallel in nature; that is, children play *next* to each other without really interacting. Even when children may be talking together, close attention reveals that they are not communicating about the same subject. One of us recently observed two toddlers busily occupied in parallel play. These children were sitting side by side on the floor, each building with blocks, and apparently engaged in an animated discussion. As odd as it may seem in an adult context, it turned out that one child was talking about his grandmother and the other about her dog. They were both playing with blocks and they were both talking, but they were not really connecting in a give-and-take manner. (Nor would we expect them to be. As we stated earlier, only toward the end of this period does cooperative play begin.)

We have labeled this period of development the "choices phase" because the best strategy for managing toddlers is to provide them with a choice of two (or more) alternatives which are acceptable to parents. We will talk more specifically about choices later in this chapter.

Normal Development: Mile Markers

In this section we explain the developmental processes and patterns typical of the toddler years: **creation of a sense of autonomy, separation/individuation, learning of self-control, symbolic thinking, self-centered point of view, over-reliance on perception, and conformity to rules to avoid punishment**. Because these are normal occurrences, we urge parents to tolerate any difficult behaviors associated with them and avoid punishment. If parents struggle with children over these issues, conflicts may persist well beyond this stage. On the other hand, patience and understanding will help children progress smoothly over any expectable bumps along the way.

Autonomy: The Development of an Independent Self

One of the most important developmental tasks for any child in this phase is the creation of a sense of autonomy or independence. Children's urge to become more autonomous is driven in part by their physical maturation and in part by the psychological need to feel proud of their emerging abilities—the "Me do it myself" need, as we have come to call it.

Anyone who spends time with toddlers will quickly recognize how pressing it is to these children to do things for themselves. This need first takes the form of determined refusals to do what someone else wants them to do. Virtually all parents of two-year-olds face a bombardment of loud "No!"s that can feel overwhelming and endless at times. However, the frequent use of "No" and strongly oppositional behavior indicate the child's growing sense of autonomy and as such are grounds for parental pride rather than dread. As was true during the earlier infant phase, development during the toddler phase proceeds in an uneven, "two steps forward, one step backward" fashion. Children normally vacillate between dependence and autonomy during this period, and sometimes even apparently minor upsets can lead to more dependent behavior. The child who insists on buttoning his own coat one day may demand that Mommy do it for him the next.

Of course, children's need to feel autonomous often exceeds their ability to act independently and competently during this period. Sometimes they are psychologically ready for increased autonomy before their emerging physical competence allows them to do what they want to do for themselves. For example, a three-year-old may want to buckle her own shoe before her fine motor skills are ready for this accomplishment. As one might imagine, children find these situations quite frustrating.

This period can prove difficult for parents as their sweet, cuddly, lovable baby increasingly transforms into a willful and sometimes unapproachable little person. Be assured that many parents feel rejected and unappreciated at times during this period. Even the most understanding and supportive parents are likely to find their patience sorely tested when their three-year-old son insists on snapping his own shirt—an endeavor which usually takes a full five minutes—when they are already late for church.

On the other hand, one of the true joys of parenthood is the opportunity to watch a child master a new skill entirely on his or her own, and to rejoice in the psychological birth of a new person.

Separation/Individuation: Learning How to Be Alone

Another significant developmental task for any child in this stage is the budding ability to separate from the mother or primary caregiver. The separation process actually begins during the preceding period, spurred on by the child's emerging ability to walk and physically move away from the parent. Children are usually very excited and happy about their new achievement, and this period can be great fun for Mom and Dad. Few parents ever forget the look on their child's face when he or she took the first steps alone.

The next phase in the separation process begins when children can walk well enough to explore the world. The continuing maturation of youngsters' sensory abilities enable them to move some distance from the mother but still maintain psychological contact with her by keeping her in sight or staying within the sound of her voice. Nonetheless, physical contact continues to be an important source of psychological comfort, and children will repeatedly walk away and then return and touch Mom to "refuel."

One of us recently watched a child nearing her second birthday as she "practiced" separating and reuniting with her mother. On this particular morning Allison would take a toy and go into the next room to play. In a few minutes, she would come running back, grab on to her mother's legs, and just stand there with her thumb in her mouth. Then, after a minute or two, she would see something that looked interesting and go running off again. This routine repeated itself until lunchtime.

By two years of age, most children have moved into the next phase in the separation process. Exploration of the world continues as social interaction with the parent intensifies. When children return to their mother, they want to talk with her and sometimes to give her objects. Not surprisingly, children in this phase become interested in playing games which involve losing and finding objects. "Hide-and-go-seek" is also a favorite pastime.

The separation process usually reaches a crisis right around two years, when children may experience intense and strongly conflicting wishes to cling to Mommy and to push her away. Parents are perceived in strongly polarized "all good" or "all bad" terms, and stranger anxiety may return. Parents should learn to expect highly variable behavior.

Although Tobin may once have been able to stay alone with other adults, he now may have difficulty when his mother leaves and become quite upset. On other occasions, when Mom is close by, Tobin may continue to "check in" with her. Reassured upon hearing her voice, he can continue to play.

The successful outcome of this developmental crisis manifests itself in children's behavior. The ability to create a mental picture of the mother or caregiver in her absence accounts for an increased tolerance for separations. Children begin to integrate good and bad perceptions of their parents and handle frustration better.

At 24 months, Zak was at the height of his separation crisis. He could not seem to decide if he wanted to be held or not. One minute he would insist upon being picked up, and the next he was wiggling and demanding to be put down. As he was a temperamentally "easy" child, his protests were rather muted, but still unmistakable. When friends of his parents visited, he would run to his mother and appear frightened, even though he had seen these grown-ups many times before.

By the time he was 36 months old, Zak seemed a different child. He played by himself for long periods of time in the back yard, running into the house periodically to tell his mother about his latest feat. He would now race to answer the door, and greet guests with a big smile. While he no longer needed to be held, he did enjoy getting a big hug from Mom and Dad before going to bed.

Development of Self-control: Learning to Hold Emotions in Check

During this period, children develop the foundation for self-control. In infancy, children are unable to separate thinking or feeling from acting; frustration or any upset feeling usually leads to crying or some other physical expression. However, with the development of language during the toddler years, children increasingly rely upon speech as a way to calm themselves and cope with negative emotions. Now that they can talk to express themselves, children can discuss doing something without actually carrying out the action.

One only has to watch toddlers to see examples of developing self-control, some of them quite entertaining. Jessica and Lisa were playing together when they began to argue over possession of a "My Little Pony." Suddenly, Jessica turned to Lisa and threatened, "Give me that pony or I'll explain it to you." Jessica's outburst demonstrates a child's attempt to use language as a way to calm herself without resorting to the action she was obviously contemplating.

What makes this situation so humorous is Jessica's precocious imitation of adult language. Parroting without understanding is common in this developmental period; as time passes, she will get better at verbalizing her feelings. During the toddler stage, even elementary attempts such as Jessica's indicate that the process of internalizing self-control is under way.

Children may even talk to themselves to maintain self-control. Three-year-old Brian was building a house out of blocks when he accidentally bumped it, and it crashed in a heap. As he began rebuilding, he said under his breath. "It's okay, you can build it again." Here again, a child used language to calm and soothe himself, repeating words he had probably heard from a parent.

The process of learning self-control is subject to the same erratic pattern as other developing abilities. One morning a child may be using words to express her anger, and that afternoon she may be using her fists. Furthermore, children vary greatly in the rate at which they gain self-control. As we will discuss later, physical expressions of anger should lead to behavioral consequences, while attempts to cope with uncomfortable feelings by talking should be encouraged and rewarded.

Our final example before leaving this topic involves a little girl with a fondness for stories who sometimes described her own play as it occurred using language from her favorite books. She was overheard to make such statements as, "'No, no,' she cried in anger." Her growing ability to use language to cope with unpleasant feelings allowed her to experience and accept anger without acting out in a hurtful manner.

Symbolic Thinking (Language): Learning to Use Words Like Everyone Else

Language abilities expand dramatically during this period. Early in the toddler phase, children often use new words in ways which strike adults as quite funny. A naked child who describes himself as "barefoot all over" is trying to master a new language concept. Toddlers' understanding of what they hear sometimes leads to interesting translations from adult to child (for instance, "the cross I bear" is translated to "the cross-eyed bear").

Children are also learning the rules of language during this period. Our language is governed by a complex grammar which most adults take for granted. While a child's mangling of the rules can be occasionally humorous, each attempt to use language represents an attempt to master those rules.

Self-centered Point of View: Seeing the World from the Child's Perspective Only

Another aspect of normal development during the toddler stage is children's inability to see the world from any perspective other than their own. One of us recently asked a little girl how many children there were in her family. Rebecca, the third of three children, replied "Two." Her embarrassed mother intervened and scolded the child for telling a "lie." Actually, Rebecca did not lie; rather, she did not count herself, for when she looks at the children in her family, she only sees the other two.

The inability to see the world from another perspective explains what some adults perceive as "selfishness" and "lack of empathy" in young children. After all, sensitivity and understanding of someone else's feelings require the ability to see situations from another's point of view. This larger focus is also essential to learning to share, something children of this age naturally find very difficult, if not impossible.

Of course, children's inability to see the world in any way but through their own eyes can be trying for parents. One of us recently saw a mother who, suffering from a bad headache, had asked her son to go outside and play quietly. A few minutes later, Alex came running into the house shouting at the top of his lungs, "Mommy, Mommy, come see the fort I built in the sandbox!" He was shocked and confused that his mother did not share his exhilaration and, to the contrary, seemed very angry with him for being so noisy. Alex expected that if he was excited, Mom would be excited too.

While most parents would appreciate their children's sympathetic response to a headache, the need to work in a home office, or the urgency of a phone call, they must take into account the limited perspective which characterizes this phase and not expect cooperation. Remember that the inability to see the world from someone else's point of view is perfectly normal in the toddler years.

The intellectual self-centeredness of the toddler can also produce more humorous situations, the kind which are savored and later recalled fondly. One little girl, who adored the children's book, *Goodnight, Moon*, was driven by her father to her grandmother's house to spend the night. As her father parked the car, the girl exclaimed: "Look, Daddy, the moon followed us all the way to Grandma's!"

Over-Reliance on Perception: The Way It Looks Is the Way It Is

A well-documented phenomenon of this period of development is children's tendency to rely on appearances when trying to decide what is real. During this phase, all children think that whatever they see is real. Adults are frequently tempted to try to "reason" with children, but try as they might, they cannot talk them out their ideas. To these children, "what you see is what you get," period.

The classic experiments of Swiss psychologist Jean Piaget best demonstrate this intriguing stage in children's thinking. Piaget presented young children with a line of five coins spaced very closely together. Another line of coins, placed beneath, appeared longer than the first because the five coins were spaced much further apart. Then he asked the children which line had more coins. The response was, "The bottom one." When asked why, they said, "The bottom line is longer so it has more."

Not satisfied, Piaget went on to repeat the experiment using containers of liquid. This time, he put equal amounts of water into a tall, slender container and into a short, wide container. Again he asked which held more, and again the children replied, "The tall one because it is bigger." This over-reliance on appearance, completely normal in the toddler years, begins to diminish around age seven, but does not totally cease until near adolescence.

The tendency to rely on what seems obviously visible to them also affects children's understanding of feelings and emotions. When their parents appear angry at them, children may find it impossible to believe that they still love them. Part of the reason for this is that children tend to see things in extremes. If Dad, visibly upset with Tricia because she disobeyed him, won't let Tricia have candy or go swimming, then Tricia may feel that he hates her. Remember, because for these children the appearance *is* the reality, it is essential that parents reassure them that Dad or Mom can be angry and still love them at the same time.

Conformity to Rules to Avoid Punishment or Consequences: Doing It Right to Keep from Getting in Trouble

During this period, children begin to understand rules of conduct and the consequences of breaking them. It is not until age seven or even older that children develop respect for rules merely because they are rules and begin to do the right thing for its own sake. In contrast, during the toddler years children do the right thing only because they remember what happens when they do the wrong thing. Moreover, parents should expect that children may not always remember. Memory is a developing and still inconsistent skill in this period. They may honestly forget things that parents find hard to believe.

Parents are sometimes needlessly concerned that they are raising a four-year-old juvenile delinquent because Mark or Katie only obeys to avoid punishment. Mark and Katie are completely normal, and every child passes through this stage. If you ask Mark, "Why should you not hit Charlie?," the answer you are likely to get is "Because I can't go to Dairy Queen." If you prompt Katie with, "Now why should you not push your sister?" she will probably reply, "Because then I can't play with her Pound Puppies." When Mark and Katie are older, they will begin to understand that hitting and pushing are not acceptable for moral reasons.

Normal Development: Preventive Maintenance

Concerned parents want to know what they can do to help their child develop normally during the toddler stage. The following section offers specific suggestions to help parents facilitate development in **autonomy**, **separation**, **self-control** and **symbolic thinking**.

Techniques to Build Autonomy

There are many ways to encourage children to become more independent. Most importantly, parents can reward children for their attempts at autonomous actions. Even when the attempt produces modest (or unsuccessful) results, a smile, an "attaboy" or "attagirl," or a big hug is just what the child needs.

Sometimes parents miss valuable opportunities to support their child's developing autonomy. We recently heard about a small boy who had gathered together paper and crayons and produced a drawing. He proudly handed it to his father, saying, "Look, Dad, it's a picture of me." The father glanced at the paper and, seeing only some crisscrossed lines, replied, "It doesn't look like you to me." Crushed, the child crumpled up his drawing and walked away, shoulders drooping. This was not a mean father, but one who focused on the accuracy of the drawing (the final product) rather than on the importance of supporting his child's efforts (the process) during this early developmental period.

Instead, the father could have helped the child by saying, "I really like your colors. Tell me about your picture. It's great! What is this part? What is that part?"

Keep this general approach in mind as you read the following list of techniques to facilitate the development of autonomy.

1. **Give choices to your child, *all* of which are acceptable to you.** Let your child decide, and then reward him or her for making a decision. For example, you can offer your daughter cookies or ice cream for dessert (if either one would be okay with you), and then praise her no matter which she chooses. Or you can ask your son if he wants milk in the blue cup or the red cup, or even to choose his own cup, if that is all right with you.
2. **Kids should be allowed to do things for themselves when they ask, and they should be encouraged to do the things for themselves that they are capable of even if they have not asked.** For example, you should tell your son: "Johnny, get the dog food can out of the cupboard and we'll open it together," or "Why don't you try to cut your cake first, and if you need help, then you can ask me."
3. **Make requests that share the responsibility between adults and children.** For example, "You get out the paper plates for our picnic, and I'll make the lemonade."
4. **Reward your child for attempts to be independent. Avoid criticizing the quality of the product of that attempt.** For example, "I like the way you combed your hair," or "You really built a high tower with those blocks."
5. **Reward your child for having his or her own ideas, regardless of how unusual they might seem.** For example, "That's a neat idea to try to make a camel out of an egg carton."
6. **Tolerate regressions (sliding back to an earlier state of development) and treat them matter-of-factly.** It is not unusual for children to overestimate their ability to do a project, and then need adult help to complete it. The best response to the cry for help is to divide the project into portions, taking the hardest parts yourself and leaving the parts that your child can do for him or her to complete, then rewarding the child for completion.
7. **Remember that any activity—no matter how small or seemingly insignificant—can be an opportunity for building autonomous behavior.** Activities can range in complexity from carrying a pencil to

Dad to planting a flower seed to spooning cookie dough onto the baking sheet.

Techniques to Build Separation/Individuation

The most powerful approach to facilitating separation/individuation in children is for the parent to remain calm, loving, likeable and predictable. During this phase, expect that a child will sometimes need to be near you, and at other times need to be away from you. Support both needs.

We advocate the following general guidelines for building separation/individuation:

1. **Let your child come to you and leave you as he or she wishes. Always keep in mind your child's emotional needs.** For example, if you allow your toddler to play in the fenced-in back yard, do not lock the kitchen door so that the child can not come in and go back out again. Recognize that the child's needs will vary from day to day or even from hour to hour. For example, a child who has been playing by herself while you iron may express a need to be held or played with. It is probably wise to stop ironing for a while and do so. Later, when the child is feeling more independent, you can resume ironing.
2. **View times when you must be away as an opportunity for your child to practice being without you. Help make those experiences positive ones.** For example, take Kelly to a weekly Mother's Day Out at the local Y, or leave Peter at his grandparents' house while you visit the dentist.
3. **Help your child adjust to the separations which you initiate by beginning with a brief period apart and gradually increasing the length of the separation.** If the child cannot calm himself or herself in your absence, reduce the length of the separation, and then gradually begin to increase it again.
4. **Give your child objects to use as memory aids to help remind your child of the person from whom he or she is separated.** These "transitional objects" can be anything which will help the child remember the absent person. We recently heard of a small girl with separation anxiety who packed a special purse to take with her to day care. The purse contained photographs of her parents and brother and family cat, as well as some favorite trinkets from home. If she missed her parents, she simply went through her purse for reassurance. The purse was very effective in helping the child to calm herself whenever the separation anxiety threatened to overwhelm her.

One of the authors of this book recently tried an even simpler transitional object. Lindsey's mother, who was leaving Lindsey in the care of the father and an uncle while she went to the store, was instructed to give Lindsey a nickel to keep in her pocket. Mom went shopping, and Lindsey was entertained by the men for a couple of hours. When she began to miss her mother and to cry for her, Lindsey was reminded to look in her pocket for the nickel that her mother had given her. She did so, and stopped crying immediately. Lindsey's Dad was impressed that something so ordinary could be so effective.

5. **Verbal reminders about the end of the parental absence are also helpful.** Before you leave, tell your child: "After Grandma gets you into bed and reads you a story, then Mom and Dad will be home to kiss you goodnight," or "After you eat dinner and feed Rover, Mom and Dad will be home to tuck you in." Remember, it is very important to do what you promise.
6. **Know that all separations are difficult for children.** Do not get upset or frustrated with your child's negative response to these changes.

Techniques to Build Self-control

The key to teaching self-control during this period, or any developmental period, is setting reasonable limits on behavior and maintaining them consistently. Both of the child's parents (and, if applicable, other important caregivers, such as grandparents) must agree upon realistic behavioral limits for the child. They should also agree about the consequences when those limits are exceeded. Then both parents can react to the same behavior in the same way.

What *is* a reasonable limit on a child's behavior? There is no single correct answer to that question. Every family will devise rules which are compatible with its own values, and those rules will vary from family to family. Within a wide range of possibilities, what is important to the child's development of self-control is not what the particular rules are, but rather, how consistently they are enforced.

We offer the following suggestions for aiding in the development of self-control:

1. **Little reminders can prove very helpful to young children who have trouble remembering limits.** One four-year-old we know liked to stand on the bottom bars of her sister's high chair. Teresa's mother, concerned that she would tip it over and both girls would get hurt, quickly got tired of telling her to get down. This mother finally

told Teresa that since she was such a big girl, she was going to teach her to read an important word. She took a large index card and printed "NO" on it and taped it to the back of the high chair as a cue. After this, Teresa rarely forgot that climbing on the bars of the high chair was not permitted. She was also pleased at herself for being able to read.

2. **Remember how reassuring behavioral boundaries are to youngsters.** Clear limits communicate to children, "I am in charge and I will not let you do anything which might hurt yourself or someone else." This message helps children to feel safe.
3. **Parents should state both limits and consequences in terms of specific actions when dealing with toddler-stage children.** You may tell your child, for example, "The bat and ball are outside toys. Take them outdoors or they will be put 'on vacation.'" Or, "When you quit jumping on the bed, then we will finish reading your story. Tell me when you are ready."
4. **When children do lose control, do *not* be angry with them.** You might want to reassure them that you understand their feelings. "It certainly is upsetting when you try to build a huge Lego tower and it falls down. I'd be upset, too."
5. **Model self-control under stressful situations.** For example, when you lose your wallet on vacation, talk through the task of finding it. "I'm sure mad that I left my wallet somewhere. Maybe it's at the restaurant. Let's call them and see."

Techniques to Build Symbolic Thinking

Many of the normal developmental phenomena discussed in the earlier section on symbolic thinking can be equally fascinating and frustrating to parents. As we indicated, children cannot be talked or trained into thinking differently; only when they have matured neurologically will their thinking be qualitatively changed. Where parents *can* make a difference, however, is in helping children begin to recognize that not everyone thinks about things in the same way.

Here are some general approaches to facilitating symbolic thinking:

1. **Parents can start teaching children the rules of language by modeling correct usage.** To the cute child who said, "Look, Mom, I'm barefoot all over," the parent could comment, "Yes, you are naked, aren't you?"

2. **Parents should also repeat and reward proper use of language.** At this stage, the goal is memorization and imitation of adult language. An understanding of the rules comes in later childhood. Therefore, parents should not punish grammatical errors or incorrect word usage. To the child's remark, "The book is them's," the sensitive parent might respond, "That's right. The book is theirs." When the child later uses correct phrasing, praise her.
3. **While it is sometimes tempting, remember not to laugh at children's language errors.** It is important to reinforce *effort* regardless of the outcome.

Staying on the Road: Choices Are Best

As we have stated, we firmly believe that parents can learn to understand why their children do what they do and use that understanding to decide on a number of possible responses to difficult or undesirable behavior. We do not think there is only one right way (and a million wrong ways) to deal with any situation. This section contains some of the management techniques which parents have found to be most successful with children during this developmental period: **choices, positive consequences, negative consequences, time-out, structure, ignoring, shaping, prompting** and **modeling.**

For more complete definitions and an overview of behavior management techniques, we refer the reader to Chapter 5.

* *Choices*

Providing children with acceptable alternatives is the most important management technique available to parents during this stage because toddlers really want and need to have some control over their world. They also need to practice autonomy and independence. Since very young children are not able to make good decisions without adult guidance, the "choices" strategy allows parents to give them exactly the kind of guidance they need by predetermining the alternatives among which the children may choose.

Someone once said, "Anything can go too far," and that is certainly true of the choices strategy. One of us consulted with a mother who was proud of how many choices she gave her child. Carl was allowed to decide on virtually every item in his own diet, without regard to inconvenience to the rest of the family. Obviously, this is not the choices strategy which we are recommending. In fact, this mother was unintentionally teaching her son that he would always be able to have whatever he wanted. Imagine Carl's anger when he eventually collides with reality.

What our overly enthusiastic mother could have done was to offer her son a choice like this one: "Would you like to have oatmeal or cold cereal for breakfast this morning?" Offering a choice that both parent and child can live with is the proper use of this management technique.

The following statements further illustrate how parents may employ the choices strategy:

> "You can play with Jennifer outside or build with blocks inside."
>
> "You can cut pictures from these magazines or read those books."
>
> "You can wear the blue shorts or the red shorts." [In this situation, a dress is not an option given to the child.]

The choices technique is amazingly versatile. There are few situations in which parents cannot come up with at least two acceptable alternatives. With time and practice, it becomes increasingly easy for parents to discover creative uses of this technique.

Positive Consequences

In order for the "positive consequences" strategy — in which rewards are contingent on a child's behavior — to work effectively during this developmental period, parents need to remember some important limitations. First, the reward component must be something the *child* wants, not something the parents think the child should want. Second, contingencies must be kept simple and should probably include some parental assistance. Finally, the child must be capable of doing the action required.

Examples of positive contingency statements made to children in this stage include:

> "*If* you try one bite of egg, *then* you may have your toast and jelly."
>
> "*When* you give Dad his glasses case, *then* he will read you a bedtime story."
>
> "*After* you flush the toilet, *then* you can go outside and play."
>
> "*If* you get the brush, *then* I will fix your hair."

One mother, having read a parenting book stressing the importance of consequences, decided to use this technique with her four-year-old. Very upset that Jeanne would not dress herself, she marched into the child's bedroom one morning and said, "You must get dressed before you child's bedroom one morning and said, "You must get dressed before you leave your room," and left. The little girl threw a world-class tantrum, and ended up crying helplessly on the floor of her room. The mother's contingency was ineffective because Jeanne had never completely dressed herself before, and she was overwhelmed by a task that was too difficult for her.

One possible solution to this mother's problem with her child would have been a series of consequences, each geared to Jeanne's current abilities. This mother could have said, "If you will put on your shirt, then I will button the buttons." Then, "If you pull on your pants, then I will zip the zipper." Next, "I will help with your socks, and then you pull on your shoes." Finally, "As soon as you put on your shoes, I will tie them, and then you can go play." It may also help you initially to provide a choice, such as "Do you want to put on your shirt or your pants first?"

Negative Consequences

Promising that some *undesirable* action will occur if a child acts in a manner that the parent finds unacceptable, "negative consequences" appropriate to this developmental stage include the following:

> "*If* you bang your new toy hammer on the furniture, *then* you will not be allowed to play with the hammer for five minutes."
>
> "*If* you pull the dog's tail, *then* we will put him outside where you can't play with him."
>
> "*If* you do not fasten your seat belt, *then* we will not go to the park."

Positive consequences are preferable to negative consequences, and should always be used if possible.

For such young children, the most effective negative consequences are those that are immediate and short-lived. As toddlers have little sense of time (each day can seem like forever), your threatening to take away a favorite weekend activity for misbehavior on a Wednesday holds no chance of affecting their behavior. Having to wait several minutes before leaving for the park because the child has hidden her shoes instead of cooperating with Mom who has been trying to dress her is about as much delay as these youngsters can understand and remember.

Time-out

For children in the toddler stage, the "time-out" technique can be used for behaviors that are dangerous or hurtful, such as banging glass containers together, hitting a sibling with a toy, or poking Dad with a pen. The length of time-out periods should range from two to four minutes, and no longer. We advise against longer periods because children's concept of time is not like that of adults. Two minutes can seem like an eternity to a small child who has been removed from a desired activity because of misbehavior and sent to a nonstimulating environment. Time-out periods longer than four minutes will be extraordinarily frustrating and lose their potency.

Although "time-out" is a powerful technique, it will not be effective if overused. We have seen occasional misuse of this strategy. For example, we were recently approached by two parents who sought consultation for their unruly three-year-old after they had implemented time-out restrictions. Conversation with the confused parents revealed that Matthew's misbehavior had led to institution of a time-out in his room which lasted from 3:00 p.m. until dinner and then from dinner until bedtime. Time-out was never intended to be used in this fashion, and is definitely not effective when implemented so extensively. If your use of time-out means that your child is spending hours in his or her room, we urge an immediate re-evaluation.

Structure

Generally speaking, structure can mean either removing temptations from a particular area or keeping the child out of an environment where bad things can happen. For example, parents can sit outside and watch their four-year-old play in the yard to avert such dangers as her running into the street or upsetting a wasp's nest, or they can put a fence around the back yard, remove dangerous objects from the fenced-in area, and allow play with minimal supervision. Erecting the fence and removing dangers from the play area are means of structuring the environment.

Sometimes structuring helps deter a nuisance rather than a real danger. For instance, if skateboards and bubbles are to be "outdoors" toys, they should be stored in the garage rather than in the child's room. Parents really cannot expect children under four to recall the rules governing the use of each toy.

Since children are developing language skills during this period, parents are tempted to try to reason with them. It is sometimes too easy to forget that these young children do not have the cognitive ability and emotional control to follow such admonitions as "You know we never (whatever) . . . because (whyever) . . . ."

Tommy, a bubbly two-year-old, was practicing his new-found ability to talk by hurrying to answer the telephone whenever it rang. This precocious child's parents were chagrined when they discovered that he frequently neglected to summon them to the phone. So they tried what they thought was the reasonable approach, and talked with the boy about the importance of getting one of them when someone called. Numerous repetitions of this discussion did not change the child's behavior. The structuring solution to this problem was so simple when it finally occurred to the parents: they moved the phone up out of Tommy's reach.

Parents may also use structuring in a positive sense. For example, to encourage creativity and fine motor skills, parents can allow the child to play with paste, paints, scissors and paper on the formica counter in the kitchen. Providing shoes with Velcro fastening and pants with elastic waistbands will make it easier for children to dress themselves and reduce frustration.

Ignoring

"Ignoring," probably one of the most important but often underutilized techniques available to parents during this period, works best when accompanied by rewards for desirable behavior. For instance, parents teaching a child to display better manners when eating will not mention the oatmeal dripping onto the chair, the salad slipping off the plate, or the child's milk mustache. When they combine this ignoring of messy eating behavior with the rewarding of neat eating habits (by smiling and making approving comments), parents can improve a child's table manners without battles during the dinner hour.

Although generally not as immediate in its effects as some of the techniques mentioned earlier, ignoring can be effective in situations where immediate change is not necessary for the child's well-being or the parent's sanity. Parents should select carefully only a few behaviors to attempt to change, and ignore most of the rest.

Shaping

"Shaping," the process of rewarding any step along the road toward the goal you want the child to reach, continues to be a worthwhile parenting strategy during this developmental period. When children first begin coloring, for example, they have little skill or control. Parents should praise them for any scribbling on the page, regardless of its relationship to the outline: "What pretty color crayons you used in this picture!" Later, parents should reward children for coloring in the area around the inside of the duck (or princess or flower) on the page: "I see you colored a duck.

parents should show that they are proud: "What a beautiful picture of a flower. You really stayed inside the lines this time!"

Prompting

"Prompting" is one of the most frequently used methods for teaching young children new behaviors. A good example is afforded by manners. Even after most young children have been reminded a thousand times to say "Thank you," they are unlikely to do so. Prompting is what mothers do when they ask a young child, "What do you say?" Manners are difficult for young children to learn because they still lack the cognitive maturity to see the world from someone else's viewpoint. Consequently, frequent prompting will be necessary until children reach a later developmental stage when they are capable of thinking about other people's feelings.

In other areas of behavior, physical prompts, such as leading the child to the bathroom at bedtime or handing her pajamas to put on, are also extremely appropriate in this phase.

Modeling

Parents "model" children's behavior by providing examples of appropriate actions that they would like children to take. Examples range from remembering to shut the door tightly when going into the backyard to starting the day with a big smile and cheerful "Good morning." In addition, Mom may comment on the attractive table Dad has set, or Dad might comment on Mom's remembering to feed the dog.

Potholes in the Road: Do-it-yourself Tune-ups

Parents of toddlers may be faced with a wide and taxing variety of "routine behavior problems." In this section we suggest ways of handling a variety of typical problems: **refusal to do tasks, separation anxiety, clinging behavior, sleep difficulties, temper tantrums, problems with sharing, fears and phobias,** and **adjustments to new situations.**

Refusal to Do Tasks (Oppositional Behavior)

Perhaps the most frequently reported problem for parents of toddlers is children's "stubbornness." Parents understandably grow impatient with their child's refusal to do what they ask. We recommend two primary strategies for dealing with these irritating and sometimes embarrassing situations: choices or consequences.

As you may recall, the choices technique involves giving a child two (or more) alternatives, either of which is acceptable to the parent. Consequences, whether positive or negative, involve a contract between parent and child in which a child's behavior has either positive consequences or negative consequences. The parent says, "*If* you do this . . . *then* I will do that . . . ." Both of these approaches have been discussed in this chapter as well as the preceding one, and the reader is referred to the relevant sections for more information.

Hard as it may be on the parents, oppositional behavior is developmentally normal for this period. "Stubbornness" does not mean that the child is "bad" or that the parent is a bad parent. Unfortunately, many parents are totally exasperated by their children's oppositional behavior, and respond in an angry way which only makes the situation worse. When a child says "No, I won't," and the parent responds with "Oh, yes, you will or I'll make you," a major battle seems about to begin. Sadly, regardless of the outcome, there are no victors, only losers. Even after the battle is over, parents experience continuing frustration over their inability to control their child, and children feel hurt because they were not allowed to exercise their growing ability to make decisions. Employing choices and consequences allows parents to exercise some control while granting the child some autonomy.

It is important to set realistic expectations for the child's behavior and to attempt to achieve an appropriate balance of control between parent and child. Parents should know that their toddler may sometimes refuse to eat peas or to kiss Grandpa good-bye, and decide that such situations are not worth fighting over. In contrast, a toddler's refusal to take medicine prescribed by the doctor requires parental intervention.

Not surprisingly, parents will survive this phase more easily with an extra dose of good humor and patience.

Separation Anxiety

Separation anxiety is common in children during the toddler phase. Since it is in this developmental period that children learn to be independent, parents should expect regressions in children's ability to cope with separations from them. One day a little boy may seem so independent that Mommy is unnecessary, while the next day he may cry at the suggestion that she go without him to the store for a few minutes. Both excessive independence and fear—as well as vacillation between them—are normal occurrences during this period.

Generally, this developmental phenomenon requires understanding and reassurance. Gradual separations from the parent with time spent with familiar persons are a good way to begin. Transitional objects may help children deal with their upset. See the discussions on facilitating separation and individuation and facilitating autonomy earlier in this chapter.

Clinging Behavior

Clinging behavior is one of the prime indications of separation anxiety. Parents can help by tolerating some clinging behavior and then actively encouraging the child to separate when the child is ready, and praising them when they accomplish this. Children cannot be ordered to be more independent. Instead, their natural inclination toward autonomy must be nurtured by understanding parents who recognize that some clinging is normal.

Children often manifest clinging behavior when they enter day care or stay with a babysitter. Several visits to the child care facility with the parent present should precede actual separations. It is important that the parent return at the designated time. For example, children will feel more secure if they know that after lunch and nap time, Mom or Dad will be there to pick them up.

Sleep Difficulties

Occasionally during this phase, children become concerned with parental separations at bedtime. We recommend that parents initiate a systematic program which involves a series of increasingly longer separations until the problem is resolved. Suppose your three-year-old daughter is raising a terrible fuss each evening at bedtime. You would go through her usual nightly routine, sit with her for ten minutes as you read a story or provide a drink of water, leave her, and return to check on her in a few minutes.

The separation interval selected should be limited enough so that the child can succeed—for example, two minutes. You continue to return until the child falls asleep. After two or three days, the interval is lengthened to perhaps four minutes. If at any point during the process the child begins to fail, fall back and make the interval shorter once again. Granted, this process takes time, but we have seen much success with it in our practices. This procedure may be enhanced by the addition of a reward such as a sticker for "staying in bed and being quiet." Because it is a positive program, it keeps upset to a minimum and promotes a more pleasant parent-child interaction.

If the child should awaken in the middle of the night, you can follow the same procedure, remaining with her for a short time and returning later to check on her.

Temper Tantrums

Toddlers are frequently frustrated little people—and for good reason. Their increasing awareness of what is possible greatly exceeds their limited abilities. Their black/white, good/bad, perfect/terrible view of the world is slowly moderated during this period to fit more closely with a gray, good and bad, mostly okay reality. However, the internal changes result from a series of collisions between the child's wishes and a sometimes painful reality. These collisions can spark temper tantrums, as children's ability to control themselves is overwhelmed by anger or disappointment that they cannot control some person or event in the way they would like.

Parents have several options when it comes to dealing with temper tantrums. **The first recommended course of action involves reassurance and labeling of feelings.** Statements such as "Boy, it's sure upsetting when you have to leave Sasha's house" or "I'd be mad too if my tricycle got stuck" are appropriate. If these measures have been utilized for a good period of time (that is, several weeks in response to the same upsetting event) with no substantial change in the child's behavior, then other techniques can be employed, including ignoring, time-out or negative consequences.

We recommend that parents begin with ignoring, as sometimes children merely need a few minutes to regain their self-control. Tantrums are only effective if there is an audience. Leave the room, informing the child, "I can see that you are upset. Take a few minutes to calm down, and then come and talk to me in the kitchen."

If the tantrums continue, then parents can introduce a program of time-out periods. It is helpful to consider time-out as an aid to the development of self-control rather than as punishment. A quiet room with little additional stimulation reduces the external demands on children's coping mechanisms, leaving them free to handle the internal distress and to resume control over their own behavior. Many child development programs use a "private" or "quiet" center, a special corner or large box where children can go on their own to gain control.

If neither ignoring nor time-out is a viable option—for example, when the child throws a tantrum at the supermarket—then parents may devise a system involving negative consequences. If, after setting up the contingency situation, the child continues with the tantrum, the parent might tell him: "You may not act this way at the store. We will have to go home now." Of course, the trick is that you have to *mean it*. In this situation, despite its inconvenience to your schedule, you must leave the grocery shopping for another time, take your child and go home.

Problems with Sharing

Many parents express concern over their toddler's unwillingness to share, not realizing that during this period of development children cannot understand the notions that underlie sharing. This is not to say that children will never share if asked. However, it is unreasonable for parents to expect toddlers to offer to share on their own or to comprehend the reason for sharing. Just because a small child shares occasionally, does not mean he or she will be able to do so consistently.

Because parents cannot expect sharing in this period, no specific management techniques are recommended. Rather, parents can structure situations to introduce the idea of sharing. For example, a parent might say: "We are going to write Kelly's name on a piece of paper and tape it to this doll. We'll let her play with the doll for five minutes. Then, you can play with it after Kelly. We'll set the timer so that you know it is your turn when the bell rings."

Fears and Phobias

The very way that children think during this period predisposes them to fears and phobias which may persist until the age of five or so. Unless the fear is so extreme as to be disabling, professional help is not required. The best strategy for the parents of a fearful child involves gradually exposing the child to the dreaded object or situation, and slowly increasing the exposure as the child's fear lessens.

Four-year-old Brent, who was afraid of the family's new pet hamster, was helped by such a systematic program. At first merely visiting the room in which the hamster was kept, Brent and his father stood or sat at a distance from the cage. The father carefully and gradually increased the time spent in the room as Brent grew more comfortable and his overt signs of fear lessened. After a few days, the viewing position was moved to the middle of the room, and the visit was lengthened. Brent's father talked to him in reassuring tones about hamsters—how soft and furry and safe they are to touch—while holding Brent to help reduce his anxiety. Next, Brent touched the hamster through the bars. Eventually, Brent actually held the pet in his hand.

Using a similar procedure, parents can help their children get over their fears. If the child should become agitated at any time during the process, the parents can comfort him or her and return to an earlier step.

Adjustments to New Situations

Children typically have difficulty adjusting to new situations during this developmental period. Their adaptability is limited by their capacity to understand the changes and by their emotional resources. At this stage, children's competency in reasoning is quite circumscribed, and their emotional resources may vary considerably from minute to minute.

Parents can help their children adjust to new situations in several ways. First, they should try to introduce children to novel experiences gradually, giving the youngsters a chance to "digest" all the different sights, sounds and smells without being overwhelmed. Second, parents should expect regressions during these transitions, and respond by being available to cuddle, talk with and comfort a shaky child. Finally, parents should avoid expecting or demanding that changes will always go smoothly or that children will automatically make quick adjustments.

New situations which young children frequently find difficult to handle include the birth of a sibling, starting nursery school, visiting in a strange home, an extended absence of parents, and going to a doctor or dentist.

Stopped on the Road: Call for Help

In this section we discuss several "serious behavior problems" which may manifest themselves during the toddler years. These behaviors fall outside the categories of normal occurrences or routine problems, and signal that professional consultation may be necessary. The serious behavior problems to be discussed are **extreme oppositional behavior, extreme phobias, refusal to separate, extreme tantrums** and **developmental delays.**

Extreme Oppositional Behavior

Some children do seem to develop extremely negative and constantly oppositional behavior during this period. If a child's behavior is characterized by temper tantrums, tears, very high activity levels and very low frustration tolerance, and this behavior persists on an almost daily basis for three to six months, parents should consult their pediatrician or a mental health professional.

Extreme Phobias

As we indicated earlier, phobias are not unusual during this period. However, if a phobia persists, unalleviated by parental efforts using the procedure described earlier, or if a phobia becomes so intense that the child's fear approaches panic, parents should seek professional advice.

Refusal to Separate

A child well beyond the age of three who clings to the primary caregiver consistently (that is, for more than a month or two) and refuses to separate for any length of time, should be referred to a mental health professional for evaluation and possible treatment. Separation anxiety may be associated with adjustment problems that warrant treatment.

Extreme Tantrums

Temper tantrums which are frightening in their intensity, occur at least daily, and persist for weeks on end, are unusual and strongly indicate the need for professional consultation.

Developmental Delays

If a child does not seem to be keeping pace with others of the same age in the development of language, speech, memory, motor skills (large or small), attention span or self-control, parents should take the child for further evaluation by a trained professional. Such developmental delays can indicate more serious psychological, physical or learning problems.

8

Early Childhood Years: "Rules Phase"

Early Childhood Years Chart

	Beginning:	Ending:
Approximate Ages:	4 Years	7 Years
Signposts:	Emergence of cooperative play	Development of ability to classify concrete objects
Normal Occurrences:	Emergence of competition Increasing interest in father Sexual identification Irreversibility of thinking Self-centered point of view Conformity for reward Socialization of behavior Learning language rules Recurrent questioning	
Primary Behavior Management Techniques: *	Positive consequences Negative consequences Time-out Reward charts Choices Modeling Structure Ignoring Prompting Shaping	

The early childhood period, which lasts roughly from ages four to seven, starts with the emergence of *cooperative* play—that is, children can interact in a give-and-take fashion—and ends as children develop a more complex *ability to classify concrete objects*. That children can now absorb new information in an organized manner may be seen in their capacity to understand categories such as animals, plants, tools or "things that are alive," "things that can be thrown," "things used for transportation," and the like. At this stage, children typically group tangible objects (things they can see and touch) rather than abstractions.

We have called this period of development the "rules phase," because the best strategy for managing children in the early childhood years is to provide them with specific guidelines which differentiate between acceptable and unacceptable behavior. We will address this topic in greater detail later in the chapter.

Normal Development: Mile Markers

In this section we explain the developmental processes and patterns typical of the early childhood years: **the emergence of competition, increasing interest in the father, sexual identification, irreversibility of thinking, continued self-centered point of view, conformity for reward, socialization of behavior, learning language rules,** and **asking recurrent questions.** Because these are normal occurrences, we urge parents to tolerate any difficult behaviors associated with them and avoid punishment. If parents struggle with children over these issues, conflicts may persist well beyond this stage. On the other hand, patience and understanding will help children progress smoothly over any expectable bumps along the way.

Emergence of Competition: "Did I Win?"

One of the most important developmental tasks for any child in this phase is the recognition of competitive feelings. Children now begin to focus on comparisons, asking such questions as:

"Is my father bigger than your father?"

"Is my dog smarter than your dog?"

"Is my dress prettier than Susan's dress?"

"Am I better at reading than Josh?"

Children's interest in answering the question, "Which is better?" stems partially from their maturing cognitive (intellectual) development which allows them to order information into classes. For the first time, children are able to determine who is taller, who can run faster, and who can sing louder. This developmental milestone frequently manifests itself in children's play. For example, a child may attempt to classify balls according to bounciness, proudly announcing which one can go higher and faster than the others.

The ability to classify concrete things in a systematic way (which is bigger, which is brighter, which is taller) has a similar impact in the social sphere. Now a child begins to wonder who in the family gets the most attention from the mother or is most appreciated by the father. In light of this development, we can easily understand children's sensitivity to the birth of siblings. In fact, children during this period may convey noticeable jealousy about parental preoccupation with other children in the family and often engage in behavior that demands parental attention. For example, four-year-old Tyson, who has been contentedly building in the sandbox by himself, may insist that his mother come look at his sand castle at precisely the same moment that she must put his younger sister down for a nap.

Children not only compete with other children but also with adults, including their own parents. We were recently told about five-year-old Carrie who ate dinner happily as long as her parents talked to her. However, the minute her parents began to discuss a grown-up subject between themselves, Carrie would no longer continue eating. Instead, she would make demands for assistance, such as "I need you to cut my meat," or "I can't reach my glass," or "I need more milk."

Increased competitiveness also revealed itself in a game initiated between Diana and her primary daycare worker. Diana would tell the adult, "I love you more," to which the other would respond, "I love you more." The game would continue ad infinitum with recurrent statements of "No, no, no, I love you more." Of course, the "I love you more" game is a highly enjoyable means of expressing and working through competitive urges.

Increasing Interest in Father: The World Grows Larger

During their earlier years, children formed a basic attachment to their primary caregiver, usually the mother. If a child has successfully separated (i.e., psychologically) from the mother and has begun to develop belief in his or her own skills and capabilities, the child is now freer to interact with the world at large.

Fathers play an important role in the separation process, partly in terms of contributing to the quality of the parents' relationship. When parents have a good relationship, the mother will tend not to be *overly* involved with the children. This helps in the mutual process of separation between child and mother.

During the early childhood period, children typically become increasingly fascinated by the father as a new and more important figure in their lives. A growing number of questions about the father and his activities is common. Kids may want to see where Dad works, learn how he earns money, find out what is in his briefcase or tool box, and so on. Even if children don't come right out and ask questions, they may imitate Dad's characteristics; a four-year-old might put on his tie or walk in his shoes, a seven-year-old may sink into "Dad's chair" with the newspaper.

Because of the high divorce rate and the shrinking number of intact nuclear families, the identity of the primary caregiver may differ from family to family. However, even in a nontraditional family structure, the pattern still holds; the child makes a transition from the single most important person to a handful of significant others. The basic sense of security established from the first attachment allows children to disengage themselves and try out new relationships.

Sexual Identification: "Am I a Boy or a Girl?"

Another important developmental process involves distinguishing between boys and girls. A child now begins to identify with the parent of the same sex—that is, to take on traits of the class labeled "male" or "female." Curiosity about sex and gender stems partially from cognitive maturation and the child's ability to divide boys and girls into separate classes. Of course, children's understanding of classes often displays some intellectual immaturity. That they may classify on a variety of different criteria was charmingly borne out by a four-year-old in our clinical practice who proudly announced to one of us that she knew the difference between boys and girls: "I can tell because boys have mustaches!"

One six-year-old we know, whose grasp of anatomical details exceeded that of the four-year-old mentioned above, was perplexed by a situation slightly beyond her comprehension. A classmate whose mother had undergone amniocentesis announced that he was expecting a baby brother. Vicky asked her own mother, "Boys have a penis and girls have a vagina, right? How do they know if the baby in Greg's mom's tummy is a boy? Did they cut her open to see?" Vicky's inability to figure out how a baby's sex could be determined without physical examination is absolutely understandable in this developmental stage. More pertinent to our discussion here, however, is Vicky's clear interest in the differences between males and females.

Children also start showing concern about gender differences in their play. When they play "house," some children assume the more traditionally masculine roles—they go out to work and earn money for the "family"—while others take on the more traditionally female roles—they prepare dinner and care for the "children." Although contemporary social circumstances have altered some of the more obvious sexual stereotyping, differentiation between men and women continues, usually reflecting family values even if the family endorses nontraditional sex roles. During the early childhood years, children often try on articles of clothing that belong to their mothers and fathers. They frequently want to wear their mommy's shoes, scarves and necklaces, or their daddy's ties and hats. Obvious physical differences between boys and girls, such as the recognition that boys have penises and girls have vaginas, often serve as the topic of conversation. Preoccupation with sexual differences is commonly expressed by playing "doctor," when children investigate the genitals of other children in an effort to determine how boys and girls differ. Children in this developmental stage typically ask repeated questions regarding bodily functions, such as "How are babies made?" Parents may want to make available books geared at the child's developmental level which discuss reproduction.

Because of children's concern with sexual identity, it is not surpising that their expressions of humor during the early childhood years tends to reflect interest in body functions. For instance, "gas" is typically met with hysterical giggles and denials of "It's not mine." (It must be the dog, the sewer or the sibling.) Children also make many jokes about the body that may be disconcerting to adults, such as "BM on you," or "You're a penis head." One can hope that these perfectly normal but potentially embarrassing (to the parent) exchanges will be kept at home—but do not be surprised when they pop up at church or the supermarket.

Irreversibility of Thinking: From Here to There, but Not Back Again

Thinking in this period is typically irreversible; that is, children think in the sequence in which activities occurred. They can recount, "We went swimming and then we went to the park, and then we went to Sarah's." It is, cognitively speaking, far more difficult to reverse the process and understand that "We went to Sarah's, before which we went to the park, before which we went swimming." This limitation presents a major impediment to logical thought which must be overcome before children can think abstractly. In practical terms, the irreversibility of thinking can account for a child's inability to respond to such questions as "Where did you lose your doll?" since kids in this stage cannot trace their steps backward in an accurate reverse order.

Continued Self-centered Point of View: "It's My World."

Children in this developmental period *cannot* fully take another's role or see another's viewpoint. They believe that everyone thinks the same way that they do. As a result, they rarely question their own thoughts because, as far as they are concerned, the only ideas possible are the ones that they hold. Thus, children's reasoning is always quite logical and correct—to *them.*

Although a normal developmental phenomenon, such limited thinking can prove frustrating for parents because their children do not respond to the parents' attempts to point out the errors in the children's logic. Not until the age of six or seven do children even recognize a conflict between their thoughts and those of their peers; children then become willing to change their own thinking because of social pressure. It is interaction with peer groups, then, rather than parental urging, which eventually jars children to question their own thinking.

We saw a child who proudly explained that he was Superman because he could lift a small chair. One of us responded, "I'm not Superman, but I think that I can lift this chair, too." This comment, clearly intended to clarify the illogicality of the child's thinking, was cheerfully ignored. As he proudly explained: "That's too bad, I got it first." While this is obviously a lighthearted example of immaturity in logical thought, similar exchanges can take place about more meaningful information, leading to upsetting disagreements between parents and children. A boy who has decided that it is not too cold to play outside without his coat on may not appreciate his mother's caution that he is likely to get sick as it is only 30°. Because the child just sees the world from his own point of view, he can easily dismiss her information and proceed in his headstrong fashion. Attempts to convince him of "facts" are destined to failure as the child *cannot* appreciate the parent's point of view. At such a time, logical discussion is an ineffective means of behavior control. Parents *must* attempt to control children's behavior by reliance on rules.

Conformity for Reward: "I'll Get Something If I Do It."

Increasingly interested in the world at large, children in early childhood develop a budding sense of self-esteem as well as a concern about rewards. Quite naturally, they learn to differentiate between behavior that leads to a positive outcome and behavior that does not. Children now typically prefer visible, concrete rewards to social approval, although they do appreciate both. However, due to a variety of cognitive limitations, children commonly perform actions based on the immediate consequences of their behavior and not because of any intrinsic motivation. During this period, a child will give a toy to another child if he or she is rewarded with M&Ms for doing so or will ask for "extra" money beyond allowance for completing chores, such as folding clothes on laundry day. The child's justification for the behavior is based on the earning of the reward—candy, money, etc.—and not on the satisfaction of engaging in a morally "good" action. Children simply lack the cognitive maturity to appreciate motivation as being important.

Children's assessment of "bad" behavior similarly reflects their intellectual limitations during this period, as many studies have shown. An adult might ask young children who was worse, a child who broke a single dish on purpose or a child who accidentally broke three dishes when he bumped into the kitchen cabinet. The typical response is that the child who broke three dishes engaged in a more serious misdeed than the child who broke only one dish. This answer clearly illustrates these children's inability to consider motivation in the judgment of behavior.

Socialization of Behavior: Learning to Live with Others

Socialization—that is, learning to live with the rules of society and adhering to them—begins at birth, of course, but children greatly expand their social interests and abilities during this developmental period.

Children must first find out what the rules are and secondly *internalize* them (understand and remember them) so that they can act in accordance with the rules under varying circumstances. As their world broadens, they begin to recognize that there are rules governing language (see below), games and social behavior.

For example, in games such as marbles, the rules are typically passed down from generation to generation. The younger child, aged four to five, does not grasp rules, and consequently plays marbles only as she understands the game. In other words, the child plays by herself; everyone can win, and no collective regulations guide behavior. (This often leads to conflicts with older siblings who voice their disgust with the "unfair" behavior and "cheating.") Around six or seven years of age, children begin to come to terms with group rules and become concerned with winning. Cooperation and adherence to complex rules appear in their games for the first time.

The learning of rules takes place in a wider arena than the playground; children learn rules at home, at school, at the store, at the community center—everywhere! They learn not to touch the perfume display at the department store, not to hit their friends, and so on. The internalization of rules is a primary developmental task in this period.

Language Rules: Learning to Talk Like Everyone Else

By the age of four or five, children become increasingly interested in communication—a process referred to as the "socialization of speech." This process involves the learning of rulcs about language as well as the *exceptions* to the rules.

Children pass through distinguishable stages in picking up language rules. For example, when younger children first start imitating adults, they may say—as would their parents—that they are putting shoes on their "feet." When they start learning rules about language, they say "feets." (After all, you make the plural form by adding an "s"—right?) Finally, when they learn about exceptions to rules, they again refer to their "feet."

Expanding Curiosity: Recurrent "Why, Why, Why?" Questions

Children's unique curiosity in the early childhood years shows up in their explosion of questions. "Why do spiders make webs?" "Why is the sky blue?" "Why do grasshoppers hop?" The barrage of questions, most of which fall into the "why" category, can literally wear out parents, who rack their brains to think up appropriate and truthful answers. Of the most typical questions in this period, many concern birth and death. The universality of the "Where do babies come from?" query may have been the inspiration for the joke about the child who came home from school wanting to know, "Where did I come from?" After the mother, squirming and thinking fast, had given him a long and involved lecture on the "birds and the bees," the boy looked at her blankly. "Haven't I answered your question?" asked the mother, praying that she had succeeded. "No," replied the child. "I meant, where did I *come* from? Charlie said he came from Cincinnati. Where did *I* come from?"

Questions about death can prove very distressing to parents. The following story illustrates youngsters' concerns in this area. Four-year-old

Kerry, who knew a girl named Buffy who had died, asked her mother how people got to heaven. The mother, recognizing her inability to explain this concept adequately to a small child, replied that she didn't know. At that moment, six-year-old Tammy piped up: "It's simple. God has a magic string. He drops it over the grave and you climb it to heaven." Three months later, the family went on vacation, flying several hours to reach their destination. When they returned, Kerry turned to her mother and said: "Remember the trip we took? I looked out of the window the whole time, but I never saw Buffy and I never saw a magic string."

That questions about birth and/or death crop up frequently does not mean that a child is obsessed with the subject. Parents can rest easy that these questions are absolutely expectable during this period. Some suggestions for dealing with them will be offered in the next section.

Normal Development: Preventive Maintenance

Parents want to know what they can do to facilitate their children's development during the early childhood years. In this section we include specific suggestions to help you support your child's growth in each of the appropriate areas—**competition, interest in the father, sexual identification, socialization of behavior, language development**—as well as ways to deal with "why" questions.

Techniques to Deal with Children's Competitive Striving

There are several ways to help a child come to terms with competition.

1. **Competition in the home environment often manifests itself in sibling rivalry.** Because this can be an issue in the early childhood years, we recommend that parents reassure their children that they love them all equally. During this period, youngsters lack the cognitive maturity to appreciate fully their parents' explanations about the disproportionate amount of time necessarily devoted to younger siblings. Nevertheless, we suggest that parents continue to explain, emphasizing that the difference in amount of time they spend with each child is not a reflection of the difference in type or quantity of love. Sometimes parents can become so engrossed in their attempts to make their children feel that they receive equal love or equal attention that the parents may fail to reinforce and encourage new achievements.

You should continue to let children know when they engage in appropriate behavior. That means telling Paul that his hair is combed neatly, that he has nice manners at the dinner table, and that he is a good helper in the kitchen. Such praise should be independent of the accomplishment of other siblings, older or younger.

2. **Children should be praised for their performance regardless of their relative standing.** The old adage, "It's not whether you win or lose but how you play the game," is particularly applicable in this developmental period. Comments such as "What a great idea to try and build a bridge to the castle" and "Boy, you sure worked a long time on that picture" are appropriate, no matter how successful the bridge or recognizable the drawing. We heard a wonderful story about a teacher who clearly shared our perspective. Seven-year-old Andrea turned in a story which was highly imaginative but contained many spelling and handwriting errors. The paper was returned with a simple "Excellent—wonderful story" written at the top of the page. Later that day, Andrea told her teacher, "Thanks, Mrs. Brewer. Next week, I'm planning to work on my spelling and handwriting."
3. **Be supportive when your child expresses disappointment over perceived competitive failures.** We recommend that parents avoid arguing with the child, saying "No, you didn't mess up." Instead, express your sympathy with such statements as "I understand your disappointment at not making the soccer goal."
4. **Do not draw attention to your child's failures** ("Remember when you struck out in t-ball?") or **emphasize another child's success** ("Frank made three home runs today—he's the best player!").

Techniques to Build Interest in the Father

As discussed earlier, during this stage children show an increasing concern with the world at large, a concern which is reflected in their growing interest in the father. The following suggestions, directed specifically at fathers, may help encourage this developmental phenomenon.

1. **You should participate in planned activities with your child,** such as going to the park on Sunday, reading bedtime stories, jogging together or building a clubhouse.
2. **You should become increasingly involved in your child's day-to-day activities,** such as attending soccer or t-ball games or helping with brushing your child's teeth.

3. **You should participate in your child's play,** particularly in activities of his or her own choosing. To build communication, you should spend a minimum of 10 to 15 minutes each day doing what the child selects without making suggestions or giving directions.

Techniques to Build Sexual Identification

As children display growing interest in differentiating between boys and girls, we encourage parents to allow them to play with specific items relevant to this classification process, such as male and female dolls. Below are several additional suggestions to help with children's sexual identification.

1. **We feel that children should be exposed to toys which allow for both more traditional male and female play *and* more cross-gender play.** Little boys should be permitted not only to play with trucks and robots but also to "cook" on the toy stove and to jump rope. Similarly, little girls can certainly play "house," but should also have trucks, cowboy gear and other stereotypically "boy" playthings and activities available.
2. **Do not punish children for playing with things traditionally assigned to the opposite sex.** We have sometimes seen fathers upset because their sons are playing with dolls. All we can say is, don't overreact; rather than indicating that these boys are "sissies," their playing with dolls is a healthy expression of their nurturing instincts. In the early childhood years, children should not be limited to specific toys or activities. Indeed, this is the stage in which to encourage them to try a variety of activities and play with toys of their choosing without adult censure.
3. **Remember that items used to help facilitate sexual identification need not be expensive or even store-bought.** Children enjoy having clothes and accessories from their parents or grandparents that they can use in symbolic play. A special "dress-up" trunk filled with discarded adult clothing, costumes and material can keep children happily and productively occupied for hours.

Techniques to Build Socialization of Behavior

Because many of the new abilities typical of this period are social in nature, children need to absorb rather quickly some rules regarding social interaction. Here are some guidelines for parents who wish to help their children learn about rules.

1. **Because rules allow children to develop a feeling of security, we recommend that parents organize family living in predictable ways.** It is reassuring for children to know that bedtime occurs at a certain hour or that Grandpa visits on Friday evenings.
2. **You should help your child to understand that certain phenomena are normal or recurrent:** the sun rises every morning, mail is delivered every day except Sunday. This helps children learn about the rules of the world.
3. **You should help children acquire experience with rules involving cause and effect.** Knowledge of specific rules, such as "If you throw pillows off the couch, then you will not sit on the sofa to watch TV" or "If you let Mommy sleep late, then you may select which TV program to watch while she is asleep" reassures children because it proves that behavior has consistent and logical consequences. (See discussions of positive consequences and negative consequence in the section on behavior management strategies.) An often overlooked fact is that adults are similarly comforted by consistency in their world. Consider, for example, a boss who is so erratic that his behavior is unpredictable from one day to another. Working for such an individual causes anxiety in adults. It therefore makes sense that erratic parental attitudes cause even more distress in children, who lack the resources to cope with inconsistency. For this reason, parents are encouraged to communicate to their children the rules by which the family structure functions on a day-to-day basis.

Techniques to Build Language Development

As noted elsewhere in this book, adults cannot force children to master language rules before they are developmentally ready. However, parents can talk and listen to their children with an interest in familiarizing them with acceptable usage. Here are some specific suggestions:

1. **You should correct children's speech to conform to common rules of grammar.** For example, if a child announces that he has "two feets," parents should accept the statement and simply restate that he has "two feet."
2. **It is important that parents perform these interventions in a non-judgmental or non-punitive fashion, not criticizing children or showing strong disapproval.** Instead, parents should pleasantly correct children's statements to help their communication approximate

adult usage. Older children occasionally correct their younger siblings in negative tones; this should be discouraged.

Techniques to Deal with Children's Curiosity

The following approaches may help parents with children's seeming endless stream of questions.

1. Parents often believe they must respond with a "because" answer, when a question actually demands a "to —" response. Following is a chart that offers "to —" alternatives as answers for "why" questions. Following the "to —" guidelines in framing answers for your child may inspire philosophical and creative responses.

Question:	Incorrect Answer	Better Answer
Why do bears hibernate?	Because they are physiologically . . . (etc.)	To get winter sleep
Why does the sun come up?	Because the earth is rotating	To help us see to play outdoors; or so plants will grow
Why do people die?	Because they get ill (or old, etc.)	To make room for other people; or because their bodies wear out

2. Once in a while most parents will need to fall back on that old standby, "Because that's the way it is." It is really difficult to provide a five-year-old with a different answer for "Why is the sky blue?"
3. An alternative to the "Because that's the way it is" answer involves asking children to come up with their own ideas: "That's a hard question. What do you think?"
4. For a youngster in this stage, the answer to "Where do babies come from?" need not entail a long discussion of eggs and sperm, but rather a brief reply starting with: "When a mother and father love each other

in a special way . . . ." However, parents who feel comfortable doing so can provide simple but concrete information, using the correct terms for body parts. Parents need to match the conceptual level of the answer to the cognitive level of the child. While you should try to be as truthful as possible, don't confuse a children with too much information or too complex a response.

5. Fortunately, not all questions are as tricky to deal with as those involving where babies come from. Questions such as "Why do I have to—?" require only a quick, "It's a (school, house, family, government) rule." Do not be afraid to use this response when it is appropriate.

Staying on the Road: Positive Consequences Are Best

As parents learn to understand their children better they can use that understanding in the development of a number of possible responses to difficult or undesirable behavior. In this section, we detail a variety of management techniques which parents have found successful with children from about age four to about age seven: **positive consequences, negative consequences, time-out, reward charts, choices, modeling, structure, ignoring, prompting** and **shaping.**

We caution you not to correct a child's every improper action for this will seriously undermine confidence. Children do not intuitively know the right way to behave, but *must be taught.*

For more complete definitions and an overview of behavior management techniques, we refer the reader to Chapter 5.

* *Positive Consequences*

The most important management technique available to parents during this period, "positive consequences" involve such "if...then" propositions as the following:

> "*If* you wait quietly for the doctor, *then* we will go out for ice cream after our appointment."
>
> "*As soon as* you get dressed, *then* you can help cut out cookies."
>
> "*When* you have brushed your teeth and are ready for bed, *then* we will read a story."

Depending upon the situation, consequences may be logical ("*When* you have cleared your dinner dishes from the table, *then* you can choose a cookie") or arbitrary ("*If* you make your bed, *then* you may invite Nathan over to play"). Logical consequences are preferable when at all possible.

As we illustrated in the previous chapter, parents must require behavior of children that they are capable of performing. For example, because children in this developmental period are unable to entertain themselves at great length, a request for a child to engage in independent, solitary play for one hour without any adult intervention would be destined to failure.

Children's preoccupation with getting what they want, or winning, is best dealt with by the creation of specific rules which outline appropriate and inappropriate behavior in a given home or school environment. Children need to know the requirements for getting what they want, and their familiarity with consequences allows them to master the social rules of the real world. Often, however, we have found that many parents have simply not conferred with one another to formulate the family rules, nor have the family rules been explained to the children. We encourage parents to determine their values regarding appropriate behavior of children in the early childhood years and to state those rules in precise terms to their child. Family rules may include the following:

- It is not okay to hit.
- It is not okay to throw toys in the house.
- You must stay seated at the dinner table until you are finished eating.
- You must be quiet when your mother is on the phone.

While many of these rules seem self-evident to adults, children cannot learn them through some intuitive process. Rather, they are aided by adults' statements of the rules and by experience with suitable consequences when the rules are disobeyed.

Children also learn rules by observing how households and schools are managed. Even with limited experience, children can reproduce the rules in similar situations. They can, for example, explain that you have recess after snack time, that you earn stickers if you finish your drawing, and that you get raisins if you play without hitting others in the playground. All these contingencies encourage the learning of rules and help children feel a sense of security. Understanding the environment as organized and systematic reassures children that they have some control over themselves and over the world around them.

Negative Consequences

Children in this developmental stage can easily understand such "negative consequences" as the following:

> "*If* you write on your bedroom set, *then* the crayons will be off limits today."
>
> "*If* you cut all the fur off of your sister's Teddy bear, *then* you will have to contribute your allowance to the purchase of a new one."

Parents should remember the following guidelines for the use of negative consequences. First, parents must consistently follow through with the promised action, or the child will soon learn to ignore these contingencies. Second, the consequence has to be undesirable *to the child.* Third, as with positive consequences, the negative consequences can be either logical or arbitrary. For instance, when a child must leave the playground because she is pushing other children, the consequence follows logically; when she must miss out on dessert because she has misbehaved at the mall, the consequence is arbitrary.

While negative consequences are helpful in managing undesirable behavior, parents are cautioned against relying upon them as their primary approach. Not only does too frequent use reduce their potency and create an unpleasant atmosphere, but it can unnecessarily increase children's frustration levels and cause the development of emotional problems. Unfortunately, our experience shows that many parents have the tendency to utilize negative consequences to the exclusion of positive ones. We believe that the frequency of positive consequences should far exceed that of negative consequences. In other words, if a child engages in unwanted activity, such as screaming while his mother is on the telephone, a positive contingency might be: "*If* you are quiet while I finish talking on the phone, *then* you can go next door and visit Johnny." In contrast, the negative contingency might consist of the following: "*If* you continue to scream and whine, *then* I will send you to the chair for five minutes." (See the section on time-out, directly below.) Whenever possible, parents should use positive consequences before negative ones.

Time-out

"Time-out," the specific negative consequence which involves removing children from an activity they enjoy to some place where they cannot perform that activity or is boring, is appropriately used in this period for dealing with dangerous, hurtful behavior as well as extremely disruptive behavior. Slapping a sibling or kicking the dog are examples.

If parents find that time-out requires too much moment-to-moment overseeing, a timer will help. The adult sets a timer as soon as the child is quiet, explaining that when it rings, the child may return to or engage in a specific activity. The child should immediately be positively reinforced for the action of "sitting quietly." In this period, time-out should range from three or four minutes to five or six minutes, and should not exceed seven minutes.

Reward Charts

A list of desired behaviors and the positive consequences their achievement will produce, "reward charts" are very useful in this phase when children begin taking responsibility for such actions as making their bed or feeding the pet. In fact, at many early elementary schools, children actually "cash in" poker chips or turn in their checked-off charts in exchange for prized items or activities. Rewards for children in the early childhood years are plentiful, ranging from a piece of candy to an extended length of time at the park to stickers or small toys. Reward charts will probably be most productive when the rewards are discussed in advance and parents take into account the child's wishes.

Choices

"Choices," a technique utilized predominantly in the preceding phase, is easily adapted for children in this developmental period. Examples appropriate to the early childhood years include these:

"You may eat your apple now or after dinner."

"You may ask Paige, Janice or Leigh to go swimming with us."

"For your birthday celebration, you may invite your friends to the pizza place, the bowling alley or to our house tonight."

Modeling

With "modeling," parents may demonstrate a particular behavior. If parents want their son to use his napkin properly during dinner, they should actually show him by example how to pick up his napkin, how to put it in his lap, and how to handle it politely during the meal. After the parents have modeled how the napkin should be used, they can verbally reward the boy for his imitation of the adults' behavior. Appropriate comments include: "That's nice, the way you wiped your mouth with the napkin," and "You did a good job folding your napkin at the end of the meal."

Structure

Discussed at length in earlier sections, "structure" remains applicable in the early childhood years. For example, if the child cannot resist fooling with the controls on the VCR, move the machine to a higher shelf beyond the child's reach or keep it locked in a cabinet. Power tools and Mom's expensive jewelry or perfume may provide similar temptations to children in this stage. Avoid unnecessary parent-child struggles by making these items inaccessible.

Ignoring

We believe when parents "ignore" undesirable behavior, it tends to wind down of its own accord. This approach continues to work well in this period for behaviors which are annoying or bothersome, such as whining and complaining, but do not present major problems at home or school.

Prompting

"Prompting," which encourages children to engage in positive behavior not occurring spontaneously, is still useful in this phase. Parents may remind a child to pick up a truck left on the living room floor, or ask, "What do we need to get ready for school tomorrow?" when the next day is "Show and Tell." Physical prompts, such as patting a chair to remind a child to stay seated at dinner, are also appropriate. Even a small gesture may act as a prompt.

Shaping

"Shaping" involves rewarding approximations of the desired behavior when the behavior in its entirety is not within the child's repertoire. For example, parents may reinforce small improvements in a child's answering the telephone politely or dressing appropriately to play in the snow until eventually the child manages to perform these actions in the hoped-for manner.

Potholes in the Road: Do-it-yourself Tune-ups

Children in the early childhood years may present many different "routine behavior problems." In this section we discuss some of these typical problems—**fighting, cheating, problems going to school, problems with siblings, disobedience,** and **overnight visits away from home**—and suggest ways in which parents may handle them.

Fighting

Parents often complain about their children's fighting. Because youngsters in this developmental phase have not learned to control their impulses at the level desired by parents, they frequently express their anger in the most immediate and direct manner: hitting, kicking, shoving, slugging, pinching, etc. Parents can help decrease their kids' fighting by explaining that such actions are unacceptable at school or at home.

We specifically recommend that children receive mild but consistent consequences for frequent fighting as this behavior appears. Time-out appears to be a particularly useful technique, as the child is separated from a group of children or sent to a corner for a few minutes to allow him a chance to calm down.

Younger children respond well to a quiet or private "center" such as a large appliance carton with a "window" and a usable "door" or a play-house. Over time, children may begin to take themselves to this area when they start to lose self-control or deliberately break a known family rule.

In the long run it may prove useful to teach children to "use your words" to defend themselves. Parents can provide kids with practice at home: "What can you say to Jeff the next time he hits you?" "How about, 'Jeff, I do not like it when you hit. I will not play with you if you hurt me on purpose.'"

We also recommend specific rewards being offered for *not* fighting. Parents should recognize and reward a child's efforts at cooperative play and "using your words" for conflict resolution.

We have spoken with parents who are concerned that their boys will not be able to protect themselves unless they learn to fight at a young age. They teach their children, "If someone hits you, you hit back!" Unfortunately, children tend to apply the rule to every situation, appropriate or not. They may hit or kick not only if attacked, but if a schoolmate accidentally shoves them while waiting for food in the cafeteria or on the pencil-sharpening line in class. Children at this stage are unable to distinguish between situations which require self-defense and those which do not. By encouraging this behavior, parents can expect to be called to conferences with school officials about their child's lack of self-control. In a much later period, children can learn to protect their rights or defend themselves in case of a physical threat. Because children lack the cognitive maturity to determine what circumstances warrant an exception to the no-fighting rule, we encourage parents to emphasize that such behavior is prohibited at all times.

We urge parents to recognize that since loss of impulse control is a common and normal developmental phenomenon in this phase, it should not warrant excessive concern unless it occurs habitually. If children fight on a daily basis and in many circumstances, then professional consultation is indicated.

Cheating

Odd as it may sound, cheating, in this particular phase, is developmentally appropriate. In other words, as children do not have the cognitive maturity with which to understand the absolute nature of rules, they often apply their own rules to a standard play situation. Again, extreme reactions are uncalled for. Rather, we encourage parents to familiarize children with the rules of the game (although children will not, at this stage, always adhere to them). However, lengthy lectures about cheating are inappropriate—to say nothing of unproductive—at this time.

Cheating is one of those developmental phenomena that require patience and understanding. Parents should know that most children will outgrow this tendency as they mature. If you must intervene, structure techniques are probably best. You may provide simple activities where rules are not involved, or have an adult play with the child so that there is adequate supervision.

Problems Going to School

During this phase of development, many children are apprehensive about school. Going to school requires sufficient emotional maturity both to allow separation from the primary caregiver and to embark on cooperative interaction with peers. As these tasks are not easy for children to master, parents need sensitivity to their children's anxieties. Parents should talk with children about school prior to their entering. When children are allowed to visit the school and meet their teacher before the first day of class, parents should take advantage of the opportunity. As time goes by, you should encourage your child to talk about any school concerns.

Again, we recommend encouragement and rewards both for attending school and for cooperative interaction with the teacher and other children. After-school treats or special activities may prove helpful. Discipline for a child's failure to perform these two acts is contraindicated, as the child's anxieties are part of the normal developmental process.

Problems with Siblings

As noted earlier in this chapter, all children have some difficulties sharing attention with their brothers and sisters. Again, this is normal. Parents may be relieved to know that squabbling, teasing and competition are perfectly normal among siblings. In fact, minor squabbling has its positive side, as it helps teach kids how to stand up for themselves, express their feelings and resolve conflicts. We recommend ignoring for this behavior.

In general, parents will best offset sibling rivalry by making each child feel loved and valued, avoiding holding one child up as an ideal, spending time alone with each child, and providing opportunities for children to be separated from each other. For harmful teasing (that is, teasing which hurts a child's self-esteem) and fighting, brief time-out procedures may be used as necessary. On the other hand, children's attempts at cooperative interaction should be rewarded.

Disobedience

Because children are just becoming familiar with rules, they usually test them to see if they are consistent predictors of behavior. Such disobedience is normal and age-appropriate. Parents need to realize that young children will require repeated exposure to the same rule to master an emotional recognition of the rule's certainty and the consistent consequences for breaking it. Rather than regard children's attempts at testing the limits as negative, parents should expect such testing and deal with it in a calm and straightforward manner.

We recommend positive consequences for obedience as the preferred method. When specific consequences are provided by the parents, they should follow through. For example, if a child is required to make the bed before playing outside, then parents must not allow exceptions. Numerous examples of such situations have been provided in previous sections.

Overnight Visits Away from Home

Having just recently completed the separation process, many children experience anxieties when visiting relatives or friends and spending the night away from home. Parents should not force children to separate until they are ready. Do test the waters; see if your child is really interested and ready to visit. If the child chooses to try spending the night away from home, the child may feel more at ease if he or she takes along a favorite toy or stuffed animal.

Once children are away, they should be encouraged to call home if they wish to make contact or verify that everything is all right. Nor should parents be surprised if their child, so eager to visit his or her friend for an "overnight," requests to be picked up in the middle of the night and taken home. Such second thoughts are quite typical in this developmental phase, and children should not be chided for "changing their minds." If parents feel they will be angry or embarrassed to make a midnight pickup, the child should simply not be allowed to go on the overnight.

Stopped on the Road: Call for Help

In this section we discuss the "serious behavior problems" which may crop up during the early childhood years. These behaviors are neither "normal occurrences" nor "routine behavior problems," and usually require professional intervention. The serious behavior problems to be discussed are **bedwetting, soiling, phobias, fire-setting, cruelty to animals, excessive anxiety, depression, developmental delays, pre-academic developmental problems, speech and language problems** and **school phobia.**

Bedwetting

A condition wherein children wet beyond the appropriate developmental period, bedwetting (enuresis) is not uncommon on an occasional basis as a response to an illness or a stressful situation, or simply as an accident. If, however, bedwetting persists several times a week for many weeks in a row, the parents should consult with their pediatrician to obtain further information on this condition and to determine if treatment is indicated.

A variety of medical and behavioral management techniques are available, including medication. A common psychological technique involves placing under the sheet a special mat which rings a bell if it becomes wet. Both medical and psychological treatments are highly successful with enuresis. Consultation can help determine if and when such approaches should be employed. Parents should be prepared, however, for many weeks of consistent effort to ensure success.

Soiling

Soiling (encopresis) is a condition in which a child continues to have bowel movements in his or her underwear, or begins doing so after being trained. We encourage parents to recognize that an occasional episode of soiling is not necessarily indicative of significant problems. However, persistent encopresis demands consultation. Mental health professionals can provide concerned parents with further information.

Phobias (After Age 5 or 6)

As noted in the earlier chapter, fears and phobias remain quite common through the age of five. Should they continue past this time and/or prove disabling, then consultation with a mental health professional is indicated. Minor fears which do not lead to major disabilities in a child's life, and therefore do not warrant consultation, include slight anxieties about adjustments to new situations and mild attempts at getting reassurance about parental absence. In sharp contrast, an absolute refusal to ride in elevators, reluctance to go under bridges for fear they may collapse, or refusal to go into school, all point to more significant distress and require consultation.

Fire-setting

Fire-setting is an extremely noteworthy behavior displayed by some children during this developmental phase. Although we cannot easily dismiss this behavior, we must stress that all children are naturally attracted to fire, often enjoying blowing out candles, or stoking campfires or the fireplace. However, playing with matches or setting a fire can have serious consequences, and consultation with mental health professionals is recommended when children who have been adequately educated and warned engage in this activity.

Cruelty to Animals

Because children do not have the cognitive maturity to empathize with others, annoying but harmless teasing of animals does occur in this period. Consultation is not necessary for this sort of behavior. Instead, it should be met with careful discussion and appropriate behavioral consequences, such as "If you pet the cat too roughly, then you may not play with her." In contrast, specific cruelty that exceeds these limits does demand professional help. In one of our practices, a parent brought in a child who had put a cat in a popcorn can, then pressed the lid tightly closed, breaking the cat's paw. This type of behavior certainly calls for professional consultation as it indicates more serious emotional distress.

Excessive Anxiety

Mild anxiety, not uncommon in this period, manifests itself in the slight fears and worries that were noted earlier, such as stage fright before a school play. However, anxiety which results in refusal to participate in usual activities for lengthy periods of time and/or refusal to perform certain tasks probably requires professional help.

Parents need to distinguish between reluctance—i.e., behavior that can be coaxed—and absolute refusal. For example, a child who is reluctant to play the piano because his playing is not perfect can often be encouraged to sit down at the piano in the living room and practice after dinner. He may even be talked into participating in his teacher's end-of-the-year recital. However, extreme anxiety could result in the child's refusing to the play piano despite coaxing. Repeated invitations to play may even result in hysterics and temper tantrums. Such behavior requires consultation.

Depression

Depression in children is a significant condition which clearly needs professional attention. As children lack the intellectual capabilities to recognize depression as a phenomenon, parents must "read" signs of unhappiness in a child's behavior. Symptoms of depression include:

1. Insomnia or other sleep difficulties
2. Low energy level or apathy
3. Persistent feelings of inadequacy
4. Decreased attention and concentration
5. Declining grades or other school problems
6. Social withdrawal
7. Loss of interest in previously enjoyed activities
8. Irritability or excessive anger
9. Inability to respond to or accept praise
10. Pessimistic attitude
11. Recurrent crying
12. Thoughts of suicide

The appearance of several of these symptoms in any combination for more than a week or two warrants professional consultation. Expressions of suicidal thought, however, always demand prompt attention.

Developmental Delays

If the child does not seem to be keeping pace with his or her age-mates in any of a variety of developmental areas (physical coordination, general information skills, etc.), comprehensive testing is indicated. These developmental delays may suggest a specific disability that warrants intervention. The parents should speak with their pediatrician and/or seek a professional evaluation to determine if developmental delays are indeed present and to explore remediation strategies.

Pre-academic Developmental Problems

When children are in preschool, they develop skills which are the precursors of later academic progress. These skills involve such areas as reading readiness, visual-motor (writing and drawing) activities and thinking. Early signs of pre-academic developmental problems often foreshadow later learning difficulties and require evaluation by professionals to determine the extent of a child's problems. Educational examiners and preschool specialists are good sources for additional information. For most children, the earlier the identification of delays and the earlier the intervention, the less disabling the problem. (See the discussion of academic delays in Chapter 9.)

Speech and Language Problems

Speech and language difficulties are best evaluated by a speech and language pathologist, although input can be provided by the pediatrician.

We must distinguish here between speech and language problems. Speech problems actually involve articulation errors, or trouble producing specific sounds. Some articulation errors are predictable, based on the child's age level. For example, many preschool children have difficulty forming the "r" phoneme, so "rabbit" is said as "wabbit." In such cases, specific intervention is not warranted. However, the same problem at a later stage may require assistance. Other problems, such as lisps, may call for further investigation. Ask your child's teacher or pediatrician for information to determine if there is a need for referral. Parents are cautioned not to correct a child's articulation errors but to provide an appropriate model instead. Drawing undue negative attention to speech errors can cause problems far more significant in nature.

Children with language problems, on the other hand, experience difficulty in mastering the rules which govern coherent language production and expanding their knowledge of words. Parents of children who have had adequate exposure to common language structures yet do not seem to be gaining proficiency are referred to speech and language professionals for information about the significance of this delay.

School Phobia

School phobia in its extreme form, such as refusal to attend school or repetitive physical complaints (with no underlying medical basis) that cause a child to spend day after day in the nurse's office, does require psychological or psychiatric help, particularly if the behavior persists. Again, mild anxieties that accompany transitions to the school environment are not uncommon, and referral should only be made if this behavior persists for more than two weeks.

9

School-age Years: "Agreements Phase"

School-Age Years Chart

	Beginning:	Ending:
Approximate Ages:	7 Years	11 Years
Signposts:	Development of concrete operational thought	Abstract thinking and entry into puberty
Normal Occurrences:	School competence Social competence Development of conscience Conformity to rules for social approval Development of thinking abilities: Seriation, classification, causality	
Primary Behavior Management Techniques:	* Social agreements Positive consequences Negative consequences Reward charts Choices Time-out Modeling Structure Ignoring Prompting Shaping	

Ranging approximately between the ages of seven and eleven, the school-age period extends from the development of the *ability to classify concrete objects* until the beginnings of true *logical and abstract thinking* as well as entry into *puberty.*

As we discussed in the previous chapter, when children first begin to develop classification schemes, they can reason logically about things that they can touch or see, such as fruit, vehicles, or fast-food restaurants. However, children's ability to think about imaginary events or abstract ideas, such as democracy or nationalism, is still limited. Only toward the end of the school-age years does this limitation begin to lift.

Signs of puberty appear at varying times for youngsters, with girls averaging their first menstruation at about twelve (although they can begin menstruating as early as ten or eleven). For boys, physical manifestations of maturing—the emergence of pubic hair and the occurrence of nocturnal emissions or "wet dreams"—tend to happen later, at about fourteen.

We have called this period of development the "agreements phase" because the primary parenting strategy involves managing children's behavior with social agreements—that is, interpersonal rewards for desired behavior. In the previous period, parenting relied heavily on the utilization of tangible rewards, such as an ice cream cone, or privileges such as staying up later than usual for a special television program. In contrast, effective parenting techniques now stress social reinforcement, including approval, recognition and praise. We will further explore these ideas later in the chapter.

Normal Development: Mile Markers

In this section we explain the developmental processes and patterns typical of the school-age years: **development of school and social competence, emergence of conscience, conformity to rules for social approval, development of thinking abilities in the areas of seriation** (putting things in order), **classification** (putting things in groups) and **causality.** Because these are normal occurrences, we urge parents to tolerate any difficult behaviors associated with them and avoid punishment. If parents struggle with children over these issues, conflicts may persist well beyond this stage. On the other hand, patience and understanding will help children progress smoothly over any expectable bumps along the way.

School Competence: "Am I Good at My Schoolwork?"

Probably the most important developmental task of the school-age years involves mastery of activities associated with the school environment. Once children have entered kindergarten or first grade, school begins to occupy a huge chunk of their waking hours. Given the time element alone, the impact of school cannot be underestimated.

The child's classroom teachers literally assume the role of substitute caregiver. A child's *positive* relationship with his or her teacher is likely to build self-esteem and self-confidence. In contrast, a child's *unpleasant* relationship with his or her teacher will probably increase the child's anxiety and internal distress.

Another major development involves a child's sense of self-esteem as related to his or her academic performance. As adults, we perhaps tend to forget the multiplicity of new tasks required during the first five years of school: participation in the first-grade activities of coloring, painting and pasting; subsequent mastery of the basics of reading, writing, spelling and arithmetic; and conformity to the social skills, work habits and attitudes of the culture or particular school environment. In each of these areas, children begin to develop a sense of their relative skill level.

Children's feeling of academic competence is based on attitudes expressed by their teachers, parents and peers. Warmth and encouragement from all three groups enhance children's positive self-esteem. On the other hand, rejection or disapproval from any one or combination of these groups is likely to have an adverse effect on children's feelings about their abilities.

Belinda felt very bad about her reading, although she possessed excellent skills. She particularly disliked reading aloud because her teacher criticized her for her very soft voice. When her parents brought the situation to the teacher's attention, the teacher changed her response to Belinda's reading aloud, becoming more encouraging and praising her for her comprehension and inflection. Belinda not only began to enjoy reading more, but frequently expressed her opinion that she was great at it.

Social Competence: "Am I Liked by My Peers?"

Another important area of growth revolves around children's relationships with their peers. Because of their egocentricism (self-focus), children in the preschool years are relatively impervious to normal pressures from their age-mates. As this focus upon the self begins to decrease somewhat in the school-age years, however, children become more susceptible to influence by their friends. For example, Lizzie's parents, who had always flooded their house and car with classical music, suddenly found their ten-year-old daughter insisting on switching the radio while car pooling to a particular rock and roll station that "everybody" listened to.

While some minor friction may result from kids' new concern with their peers, peer influence is not necessarily bad. Peer groups do provide vital opportunities for children to learn how to act with age-mates, deal with hostility, handle dominance and assume leadership.

Certain characteristics in children are likely to enhance their social status with peers. Children who succeed with other children tend to show strong attributes such as leadership, enthusiasm and active participation, or other traits such as a cheerful disposition and a friendly attitude. The characteristics associated with low social status include anxiety, emotional dependence on adults, uncertainty, withdrawal, rebelliousness and aggressiveness.

Children in this period of development are quite attuned to reactions from their peers. As we've seen in our clinical practice, children as young as five or six years of age can differentiate between "popular" and "not popular" and place themselves on a continuum of likeability. By the time they reach eight or ten years of age, they have developed a real sensitivity to status among their peers.

Eva, a bright but reticent girl, was urged by her mother to make friends in her second grade class. When asked which girls she especially liked and would enjoy playing with during recess, Eva replied "Debbie, but she's too popular. She wouldn't have time for me." Obviously, status in social groups is a highly important variable in the development of self-esteem and self-confidence. Unfortunately, it can sometimes interfere with children's willingness to engage in certain activities, form friendships or join groups.

Development of Conscience: "What Do I Think Is Right?"

Conscience, the sense of what is right or wrong in one's conduct, begins to take a new turn in this period. Children's notions of morality become easily recognizable to parents and other adults through their behavior and their explanations of why they take certain actions. For the first time, children begin to develop their own ideas about what to do and to differentiate these ideas from those of others.

Identification with parents is one factor in the development of conscience. Not surprisingly, children are more likely to identify with warm and nurturing parents. In addition, they will probably embrace parental values if they do not fear the loss of love from their parents regardless of which values they do adopt. Significantly, children who have a strong sense of conscience typically come from families that are less likely to use physical threats, force or deprivation than to use more thoughtful and understanding management of disapproved-of behavior.

Parents who discuss their children's misbehavior with them are more likely to provide children with a clear understanding of what they did wrong, thereby encouraging their children's moral development. Remember, however, that telling a child what is wrong does not necessarily communicate what is right.

Conformity to Rules for Social Approval: "I Did It So They Would Be Pleased with Me."

Ideas about conformity are closely associated with the development of conscience. In the earlier phases of development, children conform to rules to avoid negative consequences. Four-year-old Joshua does not kick the dog because he might be sent to his room; five-year-old Cathy does not pour her milk on the floor because she would have to stop to clean it up and then get dessert later than everyone else. In contrast, conformity in the school-age period occurs more often to obtain positive responses from others. For example, eight-year-old Leanne might make her bed while visiting Grandma just because Grandma likes neat rooms.

In general terms, because the child is now less egocentric and enjoys increased interactions with others, the *reason* behind conformity undergoes a shift. Expanding their social world to include teachers and peers in addition to parents, children strive to please those around them and avoid disapproval. A generalization from *concrete* rewards to *social* rewards has taken place. In the school environment, for example, children now work not only to earn stickers, but also to hear their teachers express pleasure with their productions. Of course, this is not to say that tangible rewards are no longer appreciated. Kids still enjoy receiving stickers, having their work displayed in the hallway, or getting their names on the "honor roll."

The school-age child's need for social approval was exemplified by nine-year-old Russ, who was seen in our clinical practice. Russ had been encouraged to smoke a cigarette by one of his peers. He thoughtfully responded by explaining that his swimming coach did not approve of smoking and would not like it if he took the cigarette.

He later reported the incident to the coach, and basked in the latter's approval.

Development of Thinking Abilities:
Seriation—"Can I Put Things in Order?"
Classification—"Can I Put Things in Groups?"
Causality—"Can I Devise an Explanation for this Problem?"

Seriation, classification and causality are three cognitive skills improving significantly during this period.

Seriation means the ability to arrange elements according to a given variable, such as length or weight. The capacity to order objects along a particular dimension develops gradually during this phase. While this skill may not seem particularly important to the casual observer, it actually accounts for children's ability to determine their own relative standing in a variety of areas. During the school-age years, children learn, for example, how to rank their classmates according to height, as well as how to position them according to such specifics as clarity of handwriting, popularity or speed of running. We stress the importance of this cognitive acquisition because it allows children to develop a sense of their own competence relative to their age-mates, and this, in part, accounts for children's sense of competence and self-esteem.

Classification is a logical operation that takes on a more complex level of functioning during this period of development. **Children can now take into consideration two kinds of classes simultaneously, and reverse the process.** For example, a child can now determine that there may be classes of different colored beads, such as brown, white, pink or green, while understanding that all the beads are wooden or plastic. This ability also manifests itself in social situations, as the child learns to classify children into groups of pretty/ugly, agile/clumsy or smart/dumb. Children can include or exclude themselves from certain groups and can place themselves in more than one group at a time. To be more specific, a child can now see himself or herself as popular but not particularly athletic, or strong but very short.

Causality, the ability to comprehend and explain cause and effect also expands greatly in this period. Researchers have asked children, "What happens to sugar after it is mixed into a glass of water?" Preschool-age children believe that the sugar simply disappears, whereas seven- to eight-year-olds realize that the sugar, having dissolved, remains in the water, even though it cannot be seen. A less formal demonstration of the development of causality may be observed in children's elementary notions of motivation. For example, a child may determine that "Clark hit Jamie because he was mad at him. Jamie took his marker." Children seek reasons for various outcomes, whether they be scientific or social. They want to figure out what caused a particular event to occur.

Normal Development: Preventive Maintenance

Below we outline some steps that caring parents can take to facilitate development in the following critical areas: **school competence, social relationships, conscience** and **thinking abilities.**

Techniques to Build School Competence

Parents can take these actions to help their children develop school competence:

1. **Both parents should be involved in their child's school activities.** At times this may include helping your child with special projects, quizzing him or her in preparation for tests, listening while the child reads aloud, or providing materials for art activities.
2. **You should reward your child for his or her efforts, not simply for accomplishments.** Employ such statements as "You tried hard. We're proud of you." The clear delineation between a child's effort and the quality of the resulting project tends to encourage sustained motivation in a youngster.
3. **You should compare a child's performance only with his or her previous performance, not that of age-mates or peers.** For example, you may want to say: "These math papers look so much better than the ones you did last month. Before, you could only add. Now you can do subtraction!" Again, this technique builds motivation in children.
4. **Make your expectations clear, matching them to the child's ability, without comparing your child to other children or to siblings.** Expectations should be specific to the child in question; you should expect a child of average intelligence to do average work, a gifted child to do above-average work, and a below-average child to do below-average work. Avoid negative comparisons, such as: "Robert was able to do multiplication when he was seven. You can only do addition and subtraction."
5. **It is important to reward children for good productions.** If your child writes an exceptional research paper or completes a creative project,

you should be sure to tell him or her that you are pleased not only with the end result, but with the careful planning and hard work.

6. **You should stress that perfection is not possible, and that mistakes are a necessary part of growing up and getting better at things.** Make sure your child understands that the reason children go to school is to learn how to read, to spell and so on, and that no one expects children to know everything or to do everything right.
7. **Maintain good communication with school personnel, letting them know that you are interested in their recommendations.**
8. **Make every effort to select and encourage a supportive school environment with warm, accepting school personnel and a positive emotional tone.**
9. **Provide a home environment that supports learning,** including a quiet spot for homework and adequate rest and nutrition.
10. **Model pride in intellectual or academic endeavors.** Let your child see you produce a paper or write an interesting letter or comment with pleasure on a book you have finished reading.

Techniques to Build Social Relationships

Parents can facilitate the development of social confidence and high self-esteem in the following ways:

1. **Support your child's participation in various activities** such as Scouts, Indian Guides, Camp Fire or organized sports.
2. **Encourage your child to invite friends over to the house.**
3. **Include your child's friends in family outings.** If you plan a trip to the amusement park, for example, have your child bring a friend along.
4. **Model good friendships with adult friends so that your child sees the benefits of close emotional ties.**
5. **Talk to your child in a positive way about how to make and keep friends.**
6. **Reward empathy and understanding as well as positive social skills.** Let your child know when he or she behaves as a "good friend" with such comments as "You're a good friend to Cynthia. You listen to her when she's sad."

Techniques to Build the Development of Conscience

Parents can help build the development of conscience and morality in children by acting in the following manner:

1. **Be warm and accepting toward your child.**
2. **Do not be harsh or punitive.**
3. **Provide simple, routine and consistent negative consequences for misbehavior, without expressing excessive disapproval.** Remember, all children make mistakes; misbehavior is a normal, expectable part of childhood.
4. **Talk to your child about the reasons why certain behaviors are unacceptable.** As discussed in earlier portions of this book, children cannot always understand why certain behaviors are all right and others are not. You must be clear in your explanations nonetheless. Statements such as "It is not okay to hit" provide a first step. Subsequent discussion, with such comments as "When you hit people, you may hurt them," helps a child formulate generalized rules of proper behavior.
5. **Model appropriate moral behavior for your child.** You can point out exemplary behavior with such statements as these: "Daddy does not go over the speed limit when driving," or "Mommy does not say mean things back to people who have hurt her feelings."
6. **Involve your child in institutions which provide education on moral rules consistent with the family code.** Activities at the church or synagogue, or through community organizations, may be helpful.

Techniques to Build Thinking Abilities

We recommend the following approaches to encourage cognitive skill development in this period:

1. **Expose your child to classification, ordering and reasoning activities.** Many commercial toys are available to help build these skills. If uncertain, you can ask a child's teacher about appropriate activities.
2. **Read to your child and expose him or her to as much information as possible.**
3. **Provide materials which feed or expand a child's specific interests.** For example, if your daughter is fascinated by electricity or wild animals, you should purchase or borrow the appropriate books, models, videotapes and toys for her. Kids love to be the "expert" in the family on a particular topic.
4. **Supply materials for experiments of interest to your child.** A child who expresses curiosity about how things grow will be thrilled by your helping her build a small garden in the backyard. If she wants to see if watermelon seeds really produce watermelons, you should let her plant the seeds. Allow your child to select some of the vegetables

to grow in your backyard garden, even if she chooses some which may fail (e.g., a plant that thrives in a warm climate when you live in a cold one).

5. **Listen to your children's ideas.** Rather than showing disapproval, you should communicate that you find your children's thoughts a serious matter, worthy of your attention and time.
6. **During this period children are busy making assessments of who is good at what.** Positive reinforcement of strengths *and* realistic appraisal of abilities are very important and satisfy the child's developing skills in classification in relation to social grouping. For instance, you may tell a child, "Yes, you are really good at mathematics and Abby is good in ballet." Children often get the message that if they are not the best in every area, they are not worthy. It may be helpful to draw on examples from the immediate family: "Daddy is an expert cook, while I do not enjoy cooking much. I am good at gardening, though."
7. **Both parents and children must accept the reality that skill levels differ among children.** Rather, they should encourage *effort* and reward relative gains in every area.

Staying on the Road: Agreements are Best

This section contains behavior management approaches appropriate to the period of development which we have labeled the "agreements phase." The techniques include positive consequences, social agreements, negative consequences, reward charts, choices, time-out, modeling, structure, ignoring, prompting and shaping. Because social agreements, frequently the strategy of choice during this phase, are an offshoot of the positive consequences method, we begin with the latter. Again, we want to emphasize that there are many behavior management techniques available to parents in any given situation.

For more complete definitions and an overview of behavior management techniques, we refer the reader to Chapter 5.

Positive Consequences

Although the function of "positive consequences" is gradually taken over by social agreements (see below), their use is still appropriate in this phase. Discussed at length in previous chapters, positive consequences show up in such statements to the child as these:

"*If* you make your bed, *then* you may go for a bike ride."

"*When* you finish your homework, *then* you can use the computer."

"*After* you clear the table, *then* you may watch television."

* *Social Agreements*

Providing children with appropriate social consequences is the most effective technique available to parents during this period. A specific form of the positive consequences strategy, "social agreements" involve interpersonal or social consequences—actions performed with a parent or peers. Examples include:

"*If* you take out the trash, *then* I'll play Uno with you this evening."

"*If* you show good manners when we visit our neighbor, *then* I'll work on the model plane with you afterward."

"*When* you put away your paints and brushes, *then* you may roller skate with Maria."

It makes sense to find out which social consequences inspire enthusiasm in your child, as an unappealing consequence obviously holds little chance of producing the desired behavior. One mother we know has initiated a "private time" with each of her daughters, asking, "After you have finished your homework and your evening chores, what would you like us to do together?" The family as a whole also has a negotiable "family time" in which they bike, swing in the backyard or play a board game.

At this stage, the child can take some responsibility for preparing for the subsequent consequence. For example, if Kayla wants to invite a friend over after she's cleaned her room, then Kayla is now capable of telephoning the friend herself without parental assistance.

We believe that the social agreement strategy is extremely well-matched to the developmental needs of school-age children as well as to the needs of parents who want to help their children grow and develop in the best possible manner.

Negative Consequences

Among the "negative consequences" parents might use in this developmental period are the following:

"*If* you hit your sister again, *then* you must leave the family room."

"*If* you pull the dog's tail again, *then* you cannot play with the dog for an hour."

"*If* you don't make your bed, *then* you cannot go to see Jimmy."

We recommend that parents use negative consequences only when positive consequences are not available.

This technique is mostly applicable in the management of resistant or avoidant behavior. It is important that children are aware of specific behaviors that parents consider undesirable. As much as possible, parents should discuss inappropriate behaviors and tell children about the consequences of such actions prior to their actual occurrence. Although parents of course cannot predict every behavioral deviation, we recommend that the family discuss general expectations during a family conference.

Reward Charts

"Reward charts," described in the preceding chapter, continue to be a useful behavior management tool in this period. Lists to be checked off by the child might include such actions as setting the table or completing homework. Rewards can take the form of small toys, hobby supplies or favorite desserts. Some children will prefer activities such as bowling, card games or family picnics.

Choices

The preferred strategy in the toddler stage, "choices" is still a viable technique in the school-age years. For example, a parent may ask, "Do you want to do your homework now, or in thirty minutes?" Parents then require that the child make a choice. If the child chooses to postpone doing homework for thirty minutes, the process will be helped by the parents setting a timer; the bell, and not the parent, then cues the child: "The bell says it is time to turn off the TV." Other examples appropriate to this period include setting or clearing the dinner table, and sorting the laundry or folding it after it comes out of the drier.

Time-out

Usually effective until age 10 or so, "time-out" entails the child's spending a specified period in a boring environment with few activities with which to amuse himself or herself. As spelled out in the previous chapter, time-out can be used for dangerous, hurtful or disruptive behaviors, ranging from playing with a paint gun to messing around in the parents' medicine cabinet to experimenting with the electric hedge trimmers.

In addition to the caution expressed in Chapter 5 against creating a situation in which children associate their room with unpleasantness, there is an additional consideration should parents rely on sending children to their room. By the time children are in this developmental phase, their rooms are often overflowing with a variety of entertaining toys, books and games. For this reason, time-out should occur in another, sparser environment, such as a guest bedroom or the study. Again, we remind parents that the time interval should be relatively short, with a general guideline of one minute for each year of the child's age; however, the total should not exceed seven minutes or so.

Modeling

The illustration of a desirable behavior, "modeling" works well in this period when accompanied by parental comments pointing out the modeled action. For example, a mother may mention the father's gracious manners upon the introduction of new neighbors. Modeling is a good means of teaching such social graces as shaking hands, looking guests directly in the eye when introduced, standing when an elder enters the room or answering the phone politely. Modeling is also a good if subtle way of reinforcing the idea of responsibility. For example, parents model responsible behavior when they mark the calendar to note birthdays, put away the lawn mower immediately after use or check that the front door is locked when leaving the house.

Structure

Parents should continue to use "structure" during the school-age years. For example, if they do not want a child to watch X-rated cable TV movies, they should put a child restriction device on the cable box. If certain computer files are off-limits, special access codes could be utilized. While the sites of possible contention may become more sophisticated as the child grows older, the basic principle—changing the environment so that a given unwanted behavior cannot occur—remains the same.

Ignoring

In our experience, "ignoring" is suitable for such irritating behavior as inappropriate use of language, mild temper outbursts, comments of disgust, complaining or physical signs of irritation. For example, a child's whiny "Gross, I don't know why we have to have broccoli" may best be dealt with by withholding acknowledgment as opposed to a more overt management technique.

Prompting

While "prompting" in its physical form, such as bodily removing a child from a room, was appropriate in early childhood, verbal prompts are more fitting in this phase of development. Verbal prompts include such remarks as:

"Chris, what did you want to say to Mr. Harris?"

"Beth, what should you do to take care of your new bicycle? I saw it outside."

"Are all your things collected for school tomorrow?"

Prompts may also take the form of written messages. For example, a note strategically placed by the phone may remind the child to say: "Gleason residence. This is Kim speaking."

Shaping

With "shaping," parents reinforce the child's steps towards a desired behavior. If a school-age child begins to engage in a polite social introduction, for example, but does not conclude it, the parent may still comment on his good initiation and encourage his progress to a more lengthy interaction later on. The parent might say to the child: "I like the way you introduced yourself, but next time try to remember to say 'Hello' and make eye contact."

Potholes in the Road: Do-it-yourself Tune-ups

School-age children may present a variety of "routine behavior problems." In this section we suggest ways in which parents may approach management of these vexing but not necessarily dangerous occurrences, including **refusal to do homework, stealing, lying, failure to follow family rules, and failure to participate in extracurricular activities.**

Refusal to do Homework

Unfortunately for parental peace of mind, anxiety and resistance over schoolwork are quite typical in children during this period of development. We recommend specific positive consequences that reward children for effort as opposed to grades. Parents could institute a reward chart which allows the child to earn a special activity or allowance. Some parents and children may prefer an informal system requiring a certain time commitment to homework on a daily basis, with particular rewards at specified periods (e.g., the end of a week). During this phase, parents may wish to help children either by reminding them when it is the agreed-upon time to begin their homework or by actually checking their work for completeness. It is also helpful for the child to feel she or he has some control over the situation. The parent can ask, "When do you want to do your homework, before you go out to play or right after dinner?" We feel that asking children to organize their schoolwork without any parental assistance is probably too demanding a task in the early part of this developmental period, although it is usually an appropriate requirement for adolescents.

Stealing

Stealing is not atypical during this stage. In fact, the literature suggests that nearly all children have at least a single incidence of theft, typically in the early school-age years. Parents should not be overly upset when they learn that their child has stolen something.

We recommend first that parents provide a negative consequence for stealing, and second, that parents discuss what will happen if the behavior occurs again. Generally, we think that the best consequences for stealing are related to the actual circumstances of the particular theft. For example, if a child steals a pack of gum from a friend, the child should be required to return the gum personally to the friend, possibly making his apologies to the family members as well. He could also pay a fine through deductions from his allowance. If no negative consequences are available which are directly associated with a particular incident, then other consequences might be invoked, such as restrictions on play time or cancelling participation in a desired activity. The negative consequences for a second incident should exceed those for the first incident.

Parents are advised against excessively severe punishments. What is necessary is that the parents be consistent in how they handle a child's stealing and remind the child of the family values.

Lying

Lying is very similar to stealing in being a normal developmental phenomenon in the early school-age years. One appropriate approach may be to discuss the situation. "Take a few minutes to think about what you are telling me," the parent might say to the child in positive and warm tones. "I will be pleased when you tell me the truth." And "Thank you for telling the truth," or "You did not tell the truth about . . . and that is not okay in our family."

Another approach involves mild negative consequences. The extent of the punishment may be modified if children report on themselves when they would not have been otherwise caught. For example, a parent could say: "You would have been grounded for one day if you had not told me, but since you did tell me, you will only be grounded for an hour." As in the case of stealing, the negative consequences for a second incident of lying should exceed those for a first incident.

Failure to Follow Family Rules

Due to their new interest in peers and their increased autonomy, children are often inclined to test the family environment to determine if, in fact, family rules are a necessary and required part of daily living. Positive consequences are appropriate for children's following family rules, while negative consequences are appropriate for infractions. For example, if a child has had a friend over when specifically told not to by the parents, some mild consequence or loss of privilege is suitable. In one family we know, if a child is not dressed and ready for the school bus and must be driven by the mother or father, the child has to pay the parent "taxi fare" out of his own allowance.

Failure to Participate in Extracurricular Activities

We recommend that parents of children in this phase of development require participation in a specific number of extracurricular activities. The number and types of activities called for are subject to individual values, but we feel that it is not wise to allow children to refuse to take part in any at all. You can help make the situation attractive by offering your children several options from which they themselves can make selections.

On the other hand, we often see children exhausted from a schedule of daily outside activities on top of school work that would tax any adult. Parents need to help children aim for a good balance.

We believe that by the time children reach age ten or eleven, parents should not require them to participate in any activities as they are more likely to rebel against such rules.

Stopped on the Road: Call for Help

In this section we discuss the "serious behavior problems" which may appear during the school-age period: **social isolation, anxiety and panic disorders, depression or suicide attempts, fire-setting, cruelty to animals, bedwetting or soiling, academic delays and somatic complaints.**

These behaviors fall outside the categories of normal occurrences or routine problems, and strongly point to the need for professional consultation.

Social Isolation

You may recall from the discussion on temperament in Chapter 2 that children are born with certain biological predispositions which influence their social relationships. Among the temperamental styles is one called "slow to warm up." "Slow to warm up" children are more timid around strangers, less likely to interact with people they do not know, and more anxious in social situations than children with other dispositions. These children do not need professional help unless they become so afraid that they begin to avoid people altogether, or their anxiety becomes incapacitating.

It is not simple shyness but rather a marked change in the quality or number of social interactions which may point to a potentially more serious problem. Examples include a child who suddenly stops playing with friends after school and begins to spend an increasing amount of time alone in her room, or a child who loses interest in activities with other children or displays an expressed lack of interest in friendships.

Children will certainly go through limited periods when they will be more interested in solitary play or activities than in being with their friends. Parents also need to remember that children at this age often collide with their friends and are ousted from the group for short periods of time. In addition, cliques frequently form and disband. A child caught in this kind of situation needs some extra understanding; his or her solitary state may not have anything to do with the child's behaving badly with friends.

These normal variations in a child's social life are not a cause for alarm. However, when a parent notices a persistent change in the child's typical social behavior, whether that change is abrupt or gradual, then consultation with a professional is indicated.

Anxiety and Panic Disorders

Anxiety is a psychological state characterized by rapid heart rate, increased muscle tension, increased perspiration and preoccupation with some upsetting event. Everyone experiences anxiety from time to time, and it usually passes rather quickly. Sometimes, however, anxiety can be nearly constant, or escalate into full-blown panic attacks. It is the chronic anxiety and the recurring panic attacks with which we are concerned here.

Parents can recognize anxiety which requires professional attention by the following features: unrealistic worry about future events, overconcern with performance, excessive need for reassurance and preoccupation with particular situations or events. Other behavior associated with severe anxiety includes frequent headaches or other physical complaints, inability to relax and being easily embarrassed.

Depression/Suicide Attempts

Depression is a mood disorder receiving increasing attention from both professionals and parents in the past few years. Although suicide is relatively infrequent in this age group, it does occur. The shock and tragedy of childhood suicide serve to remind us all of the difficulty of detecting depression in children.

Very few children voice feelings of being "depressed." Rather, they are likely to manifest the symptoms of depression, leaving parents to figure out what the symptoms mean and get professional help. Symptoms of depression include:

1. Insomnia or other sleep difficulties
2. Low energy level or apathy
3. Persistent feelings of inadequacy
4. Decreased attention and concentration
5. Declining grades or other school problems
6. Social withdrawal
7. Loss of interest in previously enjoyed activities
8. Irritability or excessive anger
9. Inability to respond to or accept praise
10. Pessimistic attitude
11. Recurrent crying
12. Thoughts of suicide

One or two of these symptoms may occur alone and disappear after a few days with little cause for alarm. However, when several of these symptoms present themselves for more than a week or two, professional consultation is warranted. Thoughts of suicide necessitate immediate action.

Fire-setting

Many school-age children are fascinated by fires and matches. Their curiosity may be increased by demonstrations in science class. Children may enjoy playing with matches, visiting the fire station, lighting fireworks or building campfires without help. Because children do not completely understand the nature of fire, they may show poor judgment around activities associated with fire. For this reason, adult supervision is always recommended.

A few children, however, are unhealthily preoccupied with fires. They may go to the fire station frequently, draw pictures of fires all the time in school and at home, or spend a great deal of time every day playing with matches or starting little fires and putting them out. In some rare cases, these children actually start a big fire in a basement or a garage. Parents should obtain consultation for any child who has started a fire and/or has a history of preoccupation with fire.

Cruelty to Animals

Along with fire-setting, cruelty to animals has long been considered one of the cardinal behaviors seen in emotionally disturbed children. Significant cruelty to animals does not mean pulling on the cat's tail or dressing the dog up in a hat and coat; it is putting a cat in a metal shipping crate and poking it until it shrieks. This behavior demands professional evaluation.

Preoccupation with injuries to animals is also cause for concern, even if never acted upon. Some children are attracted to the dead squirrel in the street, or the dying bird in the yard. Although this may be fairly typical behavior in three- to five-year-olds who are struggling to understand life and death, when older children seem to resonate to these kinds of events, parents need to find out what else is going on with their child.

During the school-age years, boys may develop a real, healthy interest in hunting, especially if someone they admire is an avid hunter. This kind of interest need not worry parents.

Bedwetting/Soiling

While bedwetting (enuresis) was once treated as a sure sign of emotional disturbance or family problems, we now know that in many cases, the causes are medical, not psychological. Consequently, for bedwetting problems, the first step is a thorough medical checkup with a pediatrician or urologist to eliminate physical causes.

If the medical examination reveals no physical cause for the bedwetting, then evaluation by a mental health professional is indicated. Recent advances in technology have resulted in the development of a mattress pad and electronic indicator system which wakes the child as soon as urine touches the pad. This type of training is usually quite effective in stopping bedwetting. Many professionals believe that behavioral help should be sought when the child (not the parent) is ready—for example, when the child wants to spend a night at a friend's house—so that there is real motivation.

On the other hand, lack of bowel control or soiling (encopresis) is almost always associated with emotional distress in children of this age. A medical checkup is always indicated first to rule out any physical cause for this behavior.

Soiling is associated with a variety of psychological problems in children, ranging from cognitive and perceptual problems to catastrophic reactions to overwhelming events in the life of the child or of the family. In any case, soiling on an ongoing basis requires professional help.

Academic Delays

By the time they are seven or eight years of age, some children are already having serious trouble in school. School difficulties are generally divided into two general classes: **learning problems** and **emotional problems.**

Many learning disabilities are not diagnosed prior to the second or third grade. Federal law has defined what a learning disability is and designated what services schools must provide for its identification and remediation. The primary component in determining a learning disability is a discrepancy between the child's expected performance based on his or her intellectual ability and the child's actual performance on standardized achievement tests. Achievement which is substantially behind the expected level may point to a learning disability.

Learning problems can be general in nature or limited to specific academic content areas. For example, one child's learning disabilities may be only in math while another experiences trouble only in reading or in oral language. Whether the problems are limited to specific areas or not, the strategy for treating them involves thorough evaluation of the child, followed by development of a special education plan to remediate the problem. (Sometimes total remediation is not possible; children with severe learning problems may always experience difficulty in their weak subject areas.) Parents have the option of having the evaluation conducted by school personnel or by a professional in the private sector. Early detection and remediation of learning problems is important, since ongoing academic frustration and failure leads to difficulties in developing self-esteem and leaves the child vulnerable to additional emotional problems in adolescence.

Below we list a number of problems causing poor academic performance and the ways in which they may be handled.

1. If the child has a specific learning disability in any area (e.g., reading, reading comprehension, spelling, math reasoning, math calculation, writing, oral communication, written expression), he or she may require specialized academic placement for all or a portion of the school day. Tutorial services may also be recommended.
2. If the child has an attention deficit disorder leading to problems in concentration, consultation and possibly medication may be indicated. However, the use of stimulant medication in older students and adults is controversial because some professionals view it as substance/chemical abuse. Therefore, parents may choose to get a second opinion to weigh the risks and benefits of such treatment.
3. If the child has inadequate study skills, specific techniques may be used to aid in time management and organization of materials, such as color-coded filing cards or note-taking practice.
4. If the child simply needs to be required to do or complete his or her work, specific behavioral management strategies may be called into play, as discussed previously.

Sometimes children fail to achieve in the academic arena due to emotional problems. Anxiety and depression may lead to a preoccupation which interferes with school performance. Again, consultation is needed. (See other sections of this chapter for specific discussions of emotional problems.)

Somatic Complaints

Some children are plagued by a seemingly endless series of bodily aches and pains. As always, the first step for any physical complaint is a visit to the pediatrician or family physician. However, if repeated trips to the doctor uncover only vague or puzzling causes for the complaints, then it is possible that the physical complaints are symptoms of emotional problems. For some children, physical complaints indicate that a significant emotional need is not being met. For others, aches and pains are signs of childhood depression. In still others, the somatic complaints are associated with chronically high levels of anxiety. In any case, if a child has a lengthy history of somatic complaints for which no viable physical cause can be found, then evaluation by a mental health professional is indicated.

10

Adolescent Years: "Reasoning Phase"

Adolescent Years Chart

	Beginning:	Ending:
Approximate Ages:	11 Years	18 Years to Mid-20s
Signposts:	Onset of puberty and emergence of abstract thought	Leaving home and financial independence
Normal Occurrences:	Development of identity Sexual maturation Interest in the opposite sex Importance of peer group Clarification of values Emergence of logical thinking Emergence of genuine empathy Recognition of ideals Conformity to avoid censure by authority	
Primary Behavior Management Techniques:	* Reasoning, negotiation and compromise Positive consequences Social agreements Negative consequences Ignoring Structure	

This period is marked at one end of the continuum by the onset of *puberty* and the emergence of the *ability to think abstractly* and at the other by the child's readiness for *self-support* and *independent living.*

While the capacity for abstract thought—that is, being able to think about ideas—usually emerges about age 11, there is no precise age for the onset of puberty. Girls have recently tended toward earlier first menstruation, with the average onset at about 12 years. It is not until about age 14 that boys experience comparable changes, the emergence of pubic hair and the start of nocturnal emissions ("wet dreams").

Adolescence ends when the child leaves the family home and becomes financially independent. For some, whose personal goals do not include high school graduation or a college education, this may be quite early. For others, who aspire to a college degree and/or graduate or professional training, adolescence may extend until they are actually in their mid- to late-twenties.

Children vary enormously in the ages at which they enter and leave adolescence. This phase of development, like the others that preceded it, is determined by the presence of physical and psychological changes, not by a particular birthday. Changes that accompany adolescence signal parents that a different style of parenting is necessary.

We have called this period the "reasoning phase" because the primary strategy for parenting should now be logical communication, with the emphasis on reasoning, negotiation and compromise.

Normal Development: Mile Markers

In this section we explain the developmental processes and patterns typical of the adolescent years: **development of identity, puberty and sexual maturation, interest in the opposite sex, importance of the peer group, clarification of values, development of logical thinking, emergence of genuine empathy, recognition of ideals, and conformity to avoid punishment by authority.** Because these are normal occurrences, we urge parents to tolerate any difficult behaviors associated with them and avoid punishment. Patience and understanding will help children progress smoothly over any expectable bumps along the way.

Development of Identity: The Consolidation of a Sense of Self

One of the most important accomplishments of adolescence is the creation of a stable sense of self, a process which parallels the early childhood differentiation between "me" and "not me." The adolescent version results in an internal picture which includes the child's self-evaluation as attractive or not attractive, smart or not smart, athletic or clumsy, sociable or isolated—or something in between each polarity. In contrast to the early childhood years when the family provides the primary source of information about a child's identity, peer-group feedback now carries the most weight. Not only does the adolescent's sense of identity spring in great part from social interactions, but teens typically "try out" different identities as they attempt to discover what "fits" and is consistent with their internal self-image.

During this period children are likely to take on negative or limiting self-perceptions based on the comments of others. These self-perceptions may last well into adulthood. For example, a young woman who sought professional consultation had been negatively—although inadvertently—affected by her mother. At 13, Myra had wanted to learn to play the piano, but her mother had told her that her fingers were too short for her ever to succeed. This distorted picture became incorporated into her identity. It was not until Myra was in her late thirties, after receiving professional help to clarify her *own* assessment of her abilities, that she found that her mother's view had been inaccurate. She began to take piano lessons and discovered not only that she was musically talented but that she thoroughly enjoyed nurturing a new facet to her identity.

In a developmental phase where the reactions of others are so deeply internalized, children's skill and performance can be greatly affected. A child who is told she is not much of a leader, for example, may persist in believing this even when adult life proves just the opposite. Despite successful managing of others at work or well-received endeavors to organize community activities, she may always question her leadership ability.

The recurrent question, "What do I look like?" and its ever-shifting answers are also essential elements in the development of self-identity. Worry about appearance, triggered by the rapid and sometimes bewildering physical changes of puberty, results in adolescents' preoccupation with their looks. Teenagers frequently spend hours in front of a mirror combing their hair, changing clothes and checking their complexions for pimples or their chin for whiskers. Although these rituals can drive parents to distraction, they constitute important and normal developmental behaviors. Apparently minor alterations in appearance sometimes lead to catastrophic reactions which strike parents as overly dramatic and irrational. The intensity of concern about looks indicates how fragile this aspect of the teenager's identity can be; a small change can make the entire picture feel different.

One other prevalent adolescent characteristic derives from the fragility of the adolescent's sense of self: the need to look and act like other teenagers. As you may recall, children begin to rely on their peers for support during the school-age years. During adolescence, that trend not only continues but strengthens so that peers become the main source of validation for the budding sense of self. Every new generation of adolescents has its own unique (to them) way of *looking, acting* and *thinking*—and all of these must differ radically from those of their parents. Ironically, adolescents achieve this separation from their parents by looking as much like each other as they can, because their own individual identities are too delicate to survive if they stand out from the peer group.

Individual differences which are obvious enough to make a child conspicuous in the crowd can prove traumatic during this phase of development. Children with physical disabilities can have an especially difficult time. Even children who may have been very well-adjusted to their particular disability during earlier phases of development may have significant trouble accepting it during early adolescence.

Another group of adolescents who often find their differences from their peers very hard to handle are the intellectually gifted. These teens sometimes choose to mask their cognitive abilities, giving in to the great temptation to act like one of the gang. Gifted children may avoid answering questions in class, keep their report cards from their friends, and even hide evidence of awards for fear of seeming too different from other kids (unless their peer group happens to value school achievement).

Most adolescents engage in "role-playing," a facet of identity development which is frequently (and sometimes irritatingly) evident to their parents. One day a rock star, the next a sports hero, or a TV celebrity or a radical dissident, children "try on" various personalities. That these identity "changes" are usually quite superficial may be obvious to adults, but go completely unrecognized by the teen. Kids react to a typical parental inquiry, "Who are you supposed to look like today?" with some variation of "How can you be so stupid? I look like Madonna. Anyone can see that!"

Adolescents tend to endorse each new identity as the "real" one, even though it completely differs from yesterday's "real" identity, and is likely to be replaced by another "real" role tomorrow. When parents point out the temporary nature of these identities, kids feel threatened because it reminds them how unsure they are about who they really are.

Puberty and Sexual Maturation: Becoming a Sexual Person and Coping with Sexual Feelings

The physical changes that accompany puberty are clearly among the most anxiety-provoking and emotionally charged developments of this phase. Rapid changes in body size and shape occur in unpredictable ways and at an uneven pace. Growth of the long bones of the arms and legs can lead to a "gangly" appearance. In fact, the commonness of some temporary coordination problems has encouraged the description of this period as the "awkward age."

Emotionally, these changes in appearance and sexual functioning are integrated into the adolescent's self-image at an uneven pace as well. Some girls, for example, are embarrassed by their new bodies and slump to minimize their height or wear baggy clothes to hide breast or hip development. Others sport tight jeans or provocative blouses to call attention to their new shape. Regardless of which approach is taken to cope with physical changes, both suggest a considerable emotional challenge. Any doubt there might be about the psychological demands associated with physical development is erased when one observes how sensitive adolescents are to comments about how they look. It is probably safer to carry nitroglycerin in your pocket than to make a comment about your adolescent's appearance.

Interest in the Opposite Sex: Expanding the Social World

Biological drives also produce an increased interest in information about sexual functioning and about the opposite sex. Both boys and girls experience sexual feelings at a level of intensity never felt before. The awareness of sexual drives can prove strange and frightening for both sexes. One adolescent recently commented while looking at a magnified photograph of human sperm: "They look like space invaders, don't they?" Sex definitely seems a little odd.

Not surprisingly, adolescents crave knowledge about anatomy and about the act of sexual intercourse. Much teenage sexual exploration stems from this curiosity. Recent surveys suggest that about half of all teens will have their first intercourse prior to graduation from high school. Most of the others will have engaged in some kissing and petting.

Developmentally, the most significant outcome of this period should not be sexual competence but rather sexual identification. It is both important and normal that adolescents reach the end of this period with a solid internal sense that "I am a male" or "I am a female." Dr. David Elkind, a renowned developmental psychologist, has written that a child is a child first and a boy or girl second, but that an adolescent is a boy or girl first and an adolescent second.

The Importance of the Peer Group: The Transfer of Primary Loyalty from Family to Friends

As the parents of any adolescent can attest, families are not as important to teenagers as they are to younger children. Although not always apparent, most adolescents do remain loyal to their families. This loyalty may no longer be evident in verbal expressions of love and affection, however.

The shift in primary loyalty from family to peers manifests itself differently for boys and girls. Boys seem to become part of an informal male group first, and then part of a mixed group of guys and gals, before pairing up with one particular girl. Girls, on the other hand, seem to develop a best friend or two, then become part of a mixed-sex group, and then date one boy.

Parents sometimes feel hurt that their adolescent children now turn first to peers in times of crisis or need. Difficult though it may be for parents to adjust to the loss of their role as primary comforter and advisor, adolescents do need to practice giving and taking in relationships outside the family.

The challenge to parents in this period involves shifting from being a full-time authority to being a full-time consultant. Parents who attempt to discourage the adolescent's normal reliance on peers find themselves increasingly alienated from their children and lacking influence over them. Parents can help their children—and themselves—by supporting their adolescents' moves toward independence and by coming to terms with their own sense of loss. Parents must watch their children say "good-bye" to them for six years or more.

Clarification of Values: Values as an Extension of the Maturing Self

The emergence of the ability to think abstractly and the drive for independence and autonomy contribute to the clarification of values during this period. Only at this point can children really consider values and ideas which differ from those espoused by their own families. For teens, value clarification—figuring out exactly what they really do believe—is essential to the consolidation of a mature sense of self.

Although a quite normal developmental process, value clarification can be trying for parents. The child who once agreed with them about everything from politics to religion may now vehemently advocate beliefs that parents find shocking. Just imagine the scene when a teenager from a politically conservative, religiously fundamentalist family comes home and announces during dinner that he is no longer sure that he believes in God and that he is considering joining the Socialist Workers Party.

Parents who fail to recognize this safe "trying on" of different values as a process necessary to normal development can bring it to a dead halt by reacting too strongly. One of the most harmful things you can do is to criticize values as they are being "test driven." The adolescent is then forced to withdraw from the family to continue this essential developmental activity, and the family loses its ability to influence the adolescent's ultimate choice of values.

In the situation cited above, the parents of the "radical agnostic" were enraged by their son's new philosophy. Dinner became a daily ideological battleground. An overload of criticism drove the boy into more and more involvement with increasingly radical groups until he was arrested for his part in an illegal activity mounted as a "political protest." This unfortunate outcome might have been avoided had the parents accepted the boy's "radical" ideas and allowed him to express and discuss them at home.

Emergence of Logical Thinking: Learning to Think and Solve Problems Like an Adult

One of the most significant developmental processes of the adolescent years is the transition to logical reasoning. Adolescents develop the biological maturity to think abstractly (that is, to think about ideas) and their ability to solve problems is greatly expanded.

The new cognitive skills show up in several different areas. Children can now engage in propositional thinking: "If A is greater than B, and B is greater than C, then A is greater than C." Verbal propositions are now also manageable: "If Helen is taller than Bob, and Sue is shorter than Bob, then Helen is taller than Sue." These sorts of logical rules form the basis for high level math and science which are part of most adolescents' school requirements.

A second new ability involves thinking about one's own thoughts. This sometimes leads to teenagers becoming preoccupied with their own ideas. At the same time, it means they can now anticipate the effect of what they say or do, which may produce either increased tact or increased manipulation of others, or both.

Third, children can now understand metaphors. "A bird in the hand is worth two in the bush" takes on a meaning that has nothing to do with birds or bushes. Thus adolescents are able to appreciate literature and the arts at a deeper level.

Fourth, adolescents can reason hypothetically. They can assume that a set of facts is true and reach logical conclusions based on those facts. A related development, the ability to entertain a set of ideas which are contrary to fact, means that they can consider such situations as the following: "If trees were made of plastic, then . . . ." or "If people could live on Mars, then . . . ." This development has practical implications, since it allows adolescents to solve problems which are important to them, such as: "If I want to buy a motorcycle, I'll have to get the money for it. I could ask my parents, but they probably won't give me the money. I can get a part-time job and make enough money to buy it."

Fifth, adolescents can now generate many possible solutions to some problems. For example, if you ask a teenager to tell you all the possible combinations of 14 different colors, she can figure out a strategy for determining the answers. As with all the new developments described above, this skill, called combinatorial logic, may not be used particularly well at first. Teenagers may come up with combinations of clothing which result in "mixed and unmatched" outfits; their throwing together friends with different interests at a party may lead to a social disaster. Parents may know before their child walks off to school in the blue striped pants and yellow and green print shirt that the combination just doesn't "work"; similarly, parents can predict that the party will not be a hit when they see the guest list. Hard as it is for parents to bite their tongue, it really is best. Children must undergo these experiences and learn for themselves which combinations work and which do not.

Usually a lot of extra patience is needed, too. The teenager who decides to take a new route home from his friend's house, wading through the lake and trudging up the road the long way round, may not be willfully late for dinner but merely trying out some new combination of approaches to get home. When he comes in all excited about his new-found route but oblivious to how much longer it has taken him, parents need to realize he is not necessarily being rebellious or inconsiderate of their dinner hour. Adolescents simply feel a big press to try new combinations.

Emergence of Genuine Empathy: Feeling for Others in a New Way

In younger children, understanding and sympathy are limited by their cognitive development. As adolescents develop the capacity to think abstractly, they also develop the wherewithal to put themselves in someone else's shoes. Adolescents can talk about a disagreement and describe both sides of the conflict accurately, even if they reject one or even both views—something younger children may find impossible.

The new ability to appreciate and feel someone else's pain sometimes manifests itself dramatically. One teenage girl we know recently watched a documentary about the social conditions and malnutrition in a third world country. Tracy became outraged at the inequity and injustice she saw. Although unprepared for this deeply felt anguish (their daughter had never been so intensely affected by a TV show before), her parents willingly listened to Tracy talk about her reactions. They helped her figure out what she could realistically do to help the plight of the people in the part of the world shown on TV.

The ability to feel empathy contributes significantly to adolescents' idealism and their attraction to social movements which champion the cause of a disadvantaged or downtrodden group.

Recognition of Ideals: Imagining Utopia Today

Now that they are able to think about ideas, adolescents can produce a mental construction of an ideal world. Inevitable comparisons between the real world and the teenager's imaginary Utopia can lead to intense frustration. Here begins a developmental conflict which most individuals do not resolve until well into adulthood, and sometimes not even then. No wonder that the first recognition of this dilemma is difficult for teens.

Conformity in Recognition of Authority: Following Rules While Acknowledging Exceptions to Rules

By early adolescence, kids recognize legitimate authority and the rules associated with it. Running a red light, stealing hub caps or hitting a peer all have consequences which may be administered by police or school officials.

In addition to recognizing legitimate authority, adolescents also have the ability to consider motive and intent as mitigating factors in determining the consequences for breaking rules. This new ability is a result of their capacity for abstract thought. Adolescents can understand that breaking the law may be morally right if someone's life depends upon it. For example, it may be perfectly okay to break a window to get to a fire alarm if a fire has started and there are no alternative means of notification.

Normal Development: Preventive Maintenance

Because adolescence is such a tumultuous period, parents often puzzle over what they can do to help their children develop normally. This section contains some concrete ideas about how parents can aid their teens to develop normally in the areas of **self-identity, sexual maturation, value clarification** and **logical thinking.**

Techniques to Build the Development of Identity

Here are some steps parents can take to help their children in identity development.

1. **Expect your adolescent to "try on" new roles.** Accept his or her new ideas as experiments, not the final product. Emphasize that while ideas in and of themselves are not dangerous, some behavior is; acceptance of new ideas does not mean there are no limits on actions. In other words, loosen the reins a little, but do not remove the bridle.
2. **Encourage and support your teenager's independent choices.** Express approval for thoughtful and/or creative problem-solving.
3. **Reinforce your adolescent's success at an activity or involvement in something he or she obviously cares about.** For example, compliment your daughter on being an outstanding physics student or your son on his football playing. Praise your child for a dramatic performance or a piece of writing for the school newspaper, even if these talents are not ones you had ever previously envisioned for your child. Let children know when they are good listeners and good friends.

4. **Try not to criticize choices made by the adolescent unless specifically asked for an opinion, either from your own perspective or that of society.** Too much criticism can alienate teenagers and interfere with their ability to come up with their own ideas.
5. **Be willing to listen to your child when he or she wants to talk to you.** Do not feel that you have to agree or to disagree. Simply help your child figure out what he or she thinks. You might tell your child, for example, "You seem to be saying that you are not sure whether it is better to go along with your friends or to stand up for what you believe."

Techniques to Build Adjustment to Sexual Maturation

The following suggestions may prove useful in easing adolescents' sexual maturation:

1. **Provide your teenager with accurate information about sexual development and sexual functioning.**
2. **Encourage your adolescent to talk to the pediatrician or family physician as an alternative to speaking with you if he or she seems uncomfortable or if you feel uncomfortable.**
3. **Be willing to listen to questions about sex and answer them if you can.** Never criticize your child for expressing curiosity about sexual matters.
4. **Encourage your child to get to know adults outside of the family—teachers, family friends, coaches or members of the clergy—who would serve as good male or female role models.**

Techniques to Build Value Clarification

We believe that these guidelines will help parents promote value clarification by adolescents:

1. **Parents who want their children to share their values must learn to listen to their adolescents' ideas and to accept them as important because they are what the teenagers believe at that time.** Listen uncritically as your child tries to sort out what he or she believes. Remember that values are in flux during this period, so do not overreact to the expression of any one particular idea.
2. **Talk openly about your values and about other people's values which differ from yours.** Offer, within a calm forum, your own assessment of a given situation and why you feel as you do.

3. **Provide opportunities for discussions of values with other adults and other adolescents through religious institutions, school, Scouts or other groups whose values you endorse.**

Techniques to Build Logical Thinking

Here are two practical suggestions for helping children develop their logical thinking ability:

1. **The best method to teach logical thinking is discussion which makes the adolescent explain the rationale ("why") for thinking whatever he or she does.** Raise questions which your adolescent must answer, such as "That is an interesting idea, but what about . . . ?"
2. **Avoid giving your child answers to questions which he or she can figure out alone with a little effort.** Help instead by suggesting ways to determine a solution. "It seems as though you have several alternatives. I am sure you will figure out the best one. Mom (or Dad) and I will be here to discuss the pros and cons, if you wish."

Staying on the Road: Negotiation Is Best

Parents who have navigated the previous phases successfully have a number of options open to them for managing their teenager's behavior. Children's developing ability to think logically means that parents can actually reason with them. (What a relief!) This section discusses those approaches which we think are appropriate to this developmental phase. In addition to **reasoning, negotiation and compromise,** we will look at **positive consequences, social agreements, negative consequences, ignoring** and **structure** as they apply to dealing with adolescents.

For more complete definitions and an overview of behavior management techniques, we refer the reader to Chapter 5.

* *Reasoning, Negotiation and Compromise*

"Reasoning, negotiation and compromise" constitute the preferred strategy for parents of children who have not had serious problems during earlier phases.

Because adolescents have a heightened need for independence and making their own decisions, they may find parental suggestions less palatable than before. Direct orders are likely to be totally unacceptable. Therefore, parents can be most helpful by providing adolescents with the opportunity to generate the options available to them, and to consider the risks and benefits of each.

During this phase, the most difficult task for parents is letting adolescents experience the consequences of their decisions (as long as those consequences do not involve serious, permanent injury to themselves or someone else). For parents who consider it their duty to protect their children from *any* harm, no matter how small, this hands-off policy can be extremely nerve-wracking.

Two areas in which negotiation and compromise can help spring immediately to mind: curfews and cars.

Curfew is the perennial battleground for parents and their adolescent offspring. Barbara's parents wanted to establish 11:00 p.m. as the time when Barbara had to be home on weekends. Barbara wanted to be allowed to stay out until one o'clock, which was the curfew most of her friends had to observe. Barbara and her parents compromised on a midnight deadline, with the understanding that if she were late, her curfew would be a half hour earlier on one weekend or two weekday nights.

Mike's parents decided that they could afford to spend $3,000 on a used car for him, but Mike had his heart set on a more expensive convertible. The three sat down and talked it over, finally agreeing that Mike would get the car of his dreams provided that he would pay for the difference in cost out of his earnings from working at a fast food restaurant. In the meantime, his parents would lend him the additional money, with a specified payback schedule.

Note that his parents did not order him to buy the bargain priced car. Instead, they pointed out to him: "If you spend X amount, then you have Y amount left for repairs and gas" and "We could lend you Z amount, if you get a job to pay us back." We caution parents as follows: if there really is a nonnegotiable limit, don't offer an apparently open-ended possibility. Be specific about how much a child can spend. We have heard of parents who tell their child to pick out whatever car he or she likes, then veto the choice because it is too expensive. Don't provide false opportunities or make car selection into a test for a child to fail.

In this section we have outlined two situations in which reasoning, negotiation and compromise worked quite well. It would be naive to assume that it is always as simple as we have depicted. Later on, we will discuss what to do when this approach fails (see the section on Authority/Rules Defiance Problems).

Positive Consequences

This strategy continues to serve as a valuable parental behavior management tool with teenage children when negotiation falters or when a child fails to keep an agreement. "Positive consequences" emerge in such statements to the teenager as:

> "*If* you complete mowing the lawn today, *then* you can have the car tonight."
>
> "*After* you load the dishwasher, *then* you may shoot baskets."

The use of such contingencies may provide one solution to problems with the telephone, a frequent area of contention between parents and teenagers. For example, parents can inform their daughter that she may have unrestricted phone privileges as long as her grades are satisfactory; falling grades will result in phone limitations until the marks are again satisfactory. Remember, once you have negotiated such an agreement, if the child does keep up her grades she must be allowed to speak on the phone within the agreed guidelines, even if this is irritating to the parents.

Positive consequences are most likely to prove successful when they have been negotiated between parents and children. If you are too authoritative in using this technique, the result may fall far short of expectations.

Social Agreements

Positive consequences of the social agreement type—with rewards of an interpersonal nature—may be particularly appropriate in this period. Examples are:

> "*When* you finish dusting the living room, *then* you can go to the mall with your friends."
>
> "*If* you walk your little sister to her friend's house, *then* I will help you with your tennis serve."

Negative Consequences

Recommended only when positive consequences are unavailable, "negative consequences" for adolescents may run along these lines:

> "*If* you do not help with the dinner dishes, *then* you may not make popcorn with your friends this evening."

"*If* you take your brother's mitt against his wishes again, *then* you will be unable to attend Saturday's baseball game."

As we have previously stated, parents should use logical rather than arbitrary consequences when possible.

Negative consequences, which should be negotiated with adolescents, are typically applicable in management of inappropriate behavior. As much as possible, parents should discuss undesirable behavior with their children and inform them of the consequences of such actions *prior* to their actual occurrence. Of course, by the time they are teenagers, most kids know what behavior the family considers acceptable.

Ignoring

We recommend "ignoring"—the limiting of attention directed to a remark or action—as the best strategy for dealing with the very provocative or rebellious, but otherwise harmless, behavior which some adolescents seem to relish. Suitable for behaviors that parents have the patience to see fade slowly, this technique might be used in cases of inappropriate language, mild temper tantrums, comments of disgust, snide remarks, physical displays of irritation, or radical hair and clothing styles.

Structure

There are still some situations in which the use of "structure" may prove an expedient means of heading off battles. For example, if an adolescent loads up on junk food in the morning instead of the healthful breakfast the parents would prefer he eat, the parents can simply clear the chips and soda from their shelves and make available a wide variety of appealing but nutritious breakfast foods. Other examples of situations in which structure is useful include locking the liquor cabinet and making the key to the grandparents' lake house unavailable unless permission is first obtained.

Potholes in the Road: Do-it-yourself Tune-ups

As was true with younger children, adolescents may manifest "routine behavior problems." In this section we discuss several of the most typical of these unpleasant but not necessarily dangerous situations and suggest how parents may best handle them. These areas include **conflicts over household chores, school difficulties, authority or rules defiance**

problems, challenges to parental values, changes to an undesirable peer group, unusual appearance and experimentation with sex, drugs or alcohol.

Conflicts over Household Chores

Because adolescents are physically and psychologically mature enough to carry out most household chores, many parents would understandably prefer to share the burdens of running the household. Mowing the lawn, ironing, loading the dishwasher or taking out the trash are among the duties commonly assigned to teenagers.

Although adolescent children *should* be assigned some chores, it is unrealistic to give them too many because life is so busy for them. Overloading an adolescent with daily chores will probably bring about extra battles between parents and child.

Parents need to establish deadlines for specified household activities, rather than expecting their teen to drop everything and comply immediately upon request. It is self-defeating to insist that they take out the trash (iron, mow or whatever) right then and there. Whenever possible, discuss and negotiate specific chores and deadlines.

School Difficulties

By the time they reach adolescence, most children feel accountable for their schoolwork. However, we strongly recommend that those parents who have continued or reverted to monitoring their child's homework now stop. At this stage, kids need the responsibility for their own school assignments, even if that means getting a few low grades before they recognize that it is really up to them.

For those teens who experience school problems in response to an identifiable stressful event, parents can help by instituting a program of positive consequences for a month or two. The program may provide just enough external support to get the temporarily overwhelmed adolescent back on track. He or she can participate in structuring the program by helping to determine what the rewards will be or deciding on the length of the evening study periods.

When conflict between parent and child makes negotiation difficult, we suggest that parents consider engaging a tutor or homework "coach." Tutors can sometimes bypass the disagreement and work out a study schedule while also providing educational guidance. Such a solution may save parents and kids a lot of anguish.

Authority/Rules Defiance Problems

Problems with authority may take the form of either verbal defiance, which is usually more of a hassle for parents than it is harmful to kids, or rebelliousness, which is acted out by breaking family or social rules. Verbal defiance is best managed by ignoring, or perhaps in some cases by negotiation, while defying a rule definitely requires negotiation.

When using negotiation to handle rule defiance, parents should involve the adolescent in the process. Parents may ask such questions as "What do we need to do to make sure that you get home at curfew?" or "What kind of time limits do you think you should have for talking on the phone?"

Sometimes parents really do set restraints or demands which are not reasonable for adolescents. Parents need to consider their own behavior. If the mother cannot adhere to three-minute phone calls herself, how can she demand that her teenager do so? Or, if the father's glove compartment is crammed full of parking tickets, perhaps he should reconsider how hard to come down on his child for getting a ticket.

At other times, there is a basic disagreement about what the rules should be. Negotiation between parents and teenagers may solve these problems to everyone's satisfaction.

When negotiation fails, parents should reinstitute a system of negative consequences. The cost for breaking rules may take various forms. In one contingency system, parents repeat the same negative consequence each time their child breaks a family rule. Another system involves graduated consequences for successive infractions. The latter should be used only in the case of serious problems, not for staying on the phone too long or misplacing the car keys. A combination of approaches is used in the following example, pertaining to a teenage girl and her 11:00 p.m. curfew. For each 15 minutes Sherry is late getting home, she gets 15 minutes deducted from her curfew the following night. However, should she be an hour late, double time is instituted. In other words, if Sherry arrives home at 12:15 a.m., she is docked an hour for the first hour late and 30 minutes for the additional 15 minutes late.

When using a negative system, parents need to try and develop consequences that affect the child, *not* the parents. (Neither the whole family nor the parents should suffer as a result of a teenager's misbehavior. In younger stages, of course, parents often received punishment along with the child: if a preschooler couldn't go to the park because he or she had disobeyed family rules, neither could the parents enjoy the outing.)

Challenges to Parental Values

We firmly believe that parents should let adolescents think about and believe in whatever they want. Not only is this consistent with our philosophy, but it is also pragmatic—no parent can control an adolescent's ideas. Thus, for parents to engage in struggles in the area of beliefs is not only fruitless, but counterproductive both to the child's development and to the maintenance of a good relationship. Trying to control an adolescent's ideas serves only to cut off discussion and negotiation. **Family rules should govern only actions, not thoughts.**

That the critical issue here concerns the behavior required by the parents, not what the child thinks, can be exemplified in the sphere of religion. Teenagers commonly go through periods of intense internal debate about their own spiritual beliefs. Sometimes they decide that they do not believe in God. At other times they are not sure what they believe, and announce that they will not attend church or synagogue until *they* are sure. Again, parents may choose from several different models for handling this situation. Parents can tell their adolescent children, "You may think whatever you like, but you must go to church," or "You may think whatever you like, and we will reach a compromise on how often you must attend church" or "All right. You may think whatever you like, and not attend church until and unless you feel ready to do so."

In a twist on this rather common situation, we recently heard about the adolescent daughter of atheist parents who wanted to participate in organized religion. Although we never discovered the outcome of this potential conflict, we would have recommended—had we been asked—that the parents select from similar options. That is, the parents could assure the teenager that she may think whatever she likes, but set up rules about behavior: she may pick a regular schedule of attending the church of her choice, or she may accompany a friend to church once in a while, or she may simply not be allowed to go to church.

Parents must truly understand their own values if they are to figure out a plan of action when their teenagers challenge their expressed philosophy and standards. Teenagers often force their parents to define their positions on issues that parents have not considered for many years.

Changes to an Undesirable Peer Group

While "trying on" different identities, an adolescent can become involved with an entirely new set of friends whose appearance, behavior or morals parents find objectionable. Parents may be tempted to try to talk their child out of associating with these new friends; if that does not work, parents sometimes forbid their child to see the undesirable peers.

In our experience, neither approach is likely to reach a satisfactory conclusion. Moreover, criticizing the new friends or forbidding a child to see them may well backfire. The teenager may be pushed into adopting more of the new values than he or she might have otherwise in order to maintain independence from the parents. In other words, parents risk increased rebellion and greater identification with the undesirable peer group if they engage their child in a struggle over the choice of friends.

Patti, an excellent student, transferred to a performing arts high school where she befriended a group which was heavily into drugs and radical thinking. Their punk attire and lack of successful academic performance did nothing to reassure Patti's anxious parents, who demanded that she no longer associate with these friends. The result was Patti's increased identification with the group. Whereas she used to prepare her homework carefully each night, now she turned assignments in late or not at all. Whereas she had previously spoken openly to her parents and basically adopted their values, now she withdraw from her family and her beliefs more closely resembled those of the group. After 18 months of family therapy, Patti resumed her previous homework schedule. Her parents no longer told her whom to see, but rather negotiated curfew times. Patti also started exchanging ideas with her parents once more. She began to evaluate her friends' behavior realistically and to make decisions about when to participate and when not to participate in the group's activities.

Obviously, we recommend that when a child picks friends to whom parents object, parents should avoid criticism and do nothing. This stage will probably pass—although it may, like Patti's, take quite a long time—if parents do not make it a knock-down, drag-out battle.

Unusual Appearance

Everyone has seen teenagers who dress outlandishly, sport green hair or paint their fingernails black. Drastic changes in appearance or dress are another manifestation of adolescents' search for identity.

We recommend the same approach to unusual appearance as we do to involvement with an undesirable peer group: parents should take minimal action. We do advocate setting some rules about dress that are limited to specific situations. For example, parents can expect that their children wear conventional clothes to a Sunday church service or to a synagogue wedding. Parents can also negotiate an agreement such as the following:

Blair need not wear a dress to school, but must wear one to visit her grandmother; Scott can wear his ragged jeans when he goes out with his friends, but not when he attends the yearly family reunion.

One of us recently heard a story about a girl in early adolescence who was determined to adopt a new and somewhat radical hair style, spiked high with the help of gel. Her mother, less than enthusiastic about Carline's hair, repeatedly insisted that she change it before going to school. After the struggle over the hair raged on for several months, the mother sought professional consultation. The recommendation was to let Carline wear her new hair style to school and see what happened. After the first day, the inventive adolescent came home crying because none of her friends liked her hair. When she returned to school the next day, her hair was back to normal.

Experimentation with Sex, Drugs or Alcohol

Adolescence is a time for experimentation with many different values and behaviors, including those involving sex, drugs and alcohol. You should expect to address the problem of your adolescent's thoughts about or even experience with sex, drugs or alcohol at some point during these years.

We are convinced that the best protection for parents and children is a relationship which not only allows but encourages teenagers to discuss sex and drug use (including alcohol) as much as they like. Parents who listen without criticizing or attempting to control will find that their children will approach them as they attempt to decide these difficult questions for themselves. Well-informed parents can provide answers, or at least volunteer to help adolescents locate the information they desire. A cooperative, problem-solving approach works best.

When adolescents raise questions that mostly concern what the family believes, parents can state their own values explicitly along with the relevant family rules. For example, some parents may discuss their own moderate approach to the drinking of alcoholic beverages and permit limited, supervised drinking in the home; other parents may express their sympathy with their teenager's desire to go along with their friends, but still prohibit drinking entirely until the child is age 18 or 21. Of course, negative consequences must be consistently enforced if adolescents violate the home rules.

When teenagers are away from home, however, parents cannot exercise control. Whatever their value system, they can either negotiate the negative consequences or offer assistance if a problem situation should arise. They may tell their child, for example, "Call me if you drink, and I'll come get you."

As it is unrealistic to anticipate that teenagers will not be exposed to drugs or to other teenagers who use drugs, parents need to determine what they want their own role to be; that is, do parents wish to enforce consequences, or to help kids in trouble? Our prejudice, as you have probably guessed, is that parents act as guides or consultants to their adolescents, and be available when a problem presents itself rather than policing the kids. Certainly, parents should think clearly beforehand about what they will do if a child does get into trouble and, if possible, discuss the subject in advance with the teenager.

Questions about sexual behavior are handled through discussion and information-sharing. A considerable body of research suggests that the more information on sexuality a child possesses, the lower the risks of unwanted pregnancy or parenthood. Well-informed parents can talk to their children about sexual activity and contraception. Parents who feel extremely uncomfortable or unable to do that can instead provide appropriate books for their children. Once again, parents should clearly explain the family values and outline the family expectations and rules regarding sexual behavior. Parents must come to terms with an unpleasant reality: it is not possible to govern completely the behavior of an adolescent. Once they accept this truth, parents can exercise some control by acting as "consultants" to their child as he or she tries to solve the moral and ethical dilemmas of adolescence.

Stopped on the Road: Call for Help

In contrast to the routine behavior problems described in the previous section, some adolescent behavior problems are classified as "serious" and require that the parents seek professional consultation. These include **severe academic problems, social isolation, sexual promiscuity, anxiety, depression, drug and alcohol abuse, and somatic complaints and serious family problems.**

Severe Academic Problems

It is not uncommon for adolescents to experience a variety of academic problems. Parents need to differentiate between difficulties that are related to the expectable struggles associated with increased academic demands and those failures due to true academic deficiencies. While the school may provide helpful information, educational testing offers the only definitive answer. Toward this end, parents may request an evaluation either through the school or through a private source. As we explained in the previous chapter, academic failure may stem from one or more of the following causes: specific learning disabilities, attention deficit disorder, inadequate study skills or emotional problems. Each of these calls for a different strategy.

We do stress that parents should obtain a clear understanding of the reason behind poor school performance, because the cause will dictate the course of appropriate action. Treating all academic problems as resulting from low motivation can have serious detrimental effects on adolescents and their families.

Social Isolation

Children during this developmental period often require time to themselves to think about many issues involved in the process of growing up. These solitary interludes can be useful and productive. However, in some cases social withdrawal may become excessive and require mental health consultation and possibly psychotherapy. The absence of close friends, failure to participate or lack of interest in required activities, reluctance to communicate with peers, removing themselves from family functions and/or a lack of enthusiasm for previously enjoyed activities all indicate excessive withdrawal.

Sexual Promiscuity

Despite parental anxiety, some sexual activity or experimentation by teenagers is expectable. It should be clearly distinguished, however, from a preoccupation with sexuality or inappropriate sexual conduct, which may spring from a larger emotional problem and demand professional consultation. Sexual activity with multiple partners in the absence of a caring relationship is a danger signal and should be investigated.

Anxiety

During the adolescent years, anxiety is expectable and indeed frequently experienced by *both* children and parents. Some adolescents experience anxiety of such proportions that it interferes with the normal developmental process. Overt phobias, visible signs of anxiety (wringing of hands, sighs, frequent tears), and/or recurrent expressed worry ("Nobody likes me," "I refuse to go to the party alone," "Something terrible is going to happen") are all indications of excessive anxiety that warrants professional intervention.

Depression

Depression is a common reaction to the stresses and worries of growing up. School failures, a romantic breakup, rejection from peers or temporary conflict in the home—almost anything can trigger depression. However, if the depression is not due to an identifiable loss or hurt, and/or it lasts for more than several weeks, then professional consultation is necessary.

Signs of depression include insomnia, low energy, poor attention and concentration, lowered school performance, social withdrawal, irritability, excessive anger, pessimism, recurrent tears and remarks about suicide.

Tragically wasteful, devastating to family and friends, teenage suicide is no respecter of class, race or religion. Suicide is more apt to occur during adolescence than at any other time in life because of the enormous amount of stress and change in this period. As you may recall from earlier chapters, multiple stress acts disproportionately to bring about anxiety or depression. Teenagers face physical change, cognitive leaps, emotional hurricanes and independence conflicts on a nearly daily basis. Sometimes it can all seem overwhelming.

Suicidal comments should always be taken seriously. Parents need to talk about their child's references to suicide rather than ignoring them. Consultation with a professional or a community mental health facility for further information is imperative when teenagers talk about suicide.

Drug and Alcohol Abuse

In our experience, few parents are aware of their teenage children's drug or alcohol problems. However, signs of lowered functioning are often evident; once observed, they should be taken seriously. **Indications of drug or alcohol abuse include frequent school absences, accidents, legal problems, violence, marked changes in attitude and mood swings.** Professional intervention is always warranted.

Somatic Complaints

When symptoms persist for more than a few days, physical complaints require medical evaluation. If the physician rules out all medical causes, psychological factors should be considered. Anxiety and stress can account for many physical problems, ranging from stomach disorders to headaches. If the somatic complaints appear to stem from psychological bases, then parents should seek therapy or counseling for their child.

Serious Family Problems

Mild family problems often crop up during adolescence as youngsters fight to establish a stable self-concept independent of their families. Teenagers frequently test family rules, express disapproval of parental values, act negatively toward family activities, criticize family members and show heightened dissatisfaction with their role in the family. However, if a teenager's attitudes and behavior cause frequent (at least weekly) fights of serious intensity that do not lessen with discussion and negotiation, then family therapy is indicated.

11

The Successful Journey: Good Parenting Benefits Both Parents and Children

Good parenting is not only easier on parents, it is terrific for kids. The benefits to children are not always obvious to parents, so we will once again use our journey metaphor, which emphasizes development as a process, to enumerate the advantages we find important.

Positive Effects for Children

If parents use effective parenting techniques, children **gain self-control, learn to soothe themselves, develop self-confidence** and **possess a greater capacity for enjoyment.**

Parents Can Do Less Driving and More Sightseeing: Children Gain Self-control

Although it would certainly make life easier for parents, children are not born with the capacity for controlling their actions in appropriate ways. This skill must be acquired as children mature. If we look at reactions to pain, for example, we can see enormous variations according to children's age. In very young children, the reaction is global, often accompanied by loud crying and obvious distress. A school-age child, on the other hand, may cry and demand attention. In adults, the usual reaction is more limited, confined to site of the pain, and the vocal response is restricted to a few choice words.

Children must experience some frustration and upset to have the opportunity to acquire internal control over their reactions to external events. They must learn that frustration is an inevitable consequence of living, one which they can tolerate without losing control of their behavior.

The Need for Daily Mechanical Maintenance Decreases: Children Can Learn to Soothe Themselves

Anyone who has had the opportunity to observe young children has probably seen examples of their learning to soothe themselves. This process initially consists of imitating the words and actions of a comforting parent; with increasing age and practice, the process soon becomes entirely internal.

An example was seen in our clinical practice. At the time she entered treatment, four-year-old Chrissie would typically became hysterical whenever she received a small cut or scratch. As her treatment progressed, she began to imitate her mother's responses to her own distress. She would play with her dolls and say, "Poor baby, your tummy hurts. It will be all right. I'll kiss it and make it better. I'll take good care of you. You'll be all right." Later, she was able to say this to herself when she fell on the playground. As she repeated the comforting words, the intensity of her misery over her own cuts and scratches gradually decreased.

That Hill Is Not So Steep: Children Develop Self-confidence

Children who live in a predictable environment begin to feel that they have some control over their world, and therefore begin to develop confidence in themselves and their abilities. Knowing what the negative consequences of a particular behavior will be increases their sense of satisfaction when they are able to avoid those consequences. As one of "our children" recently reported, "I had sad feelings. I cried, but I didn't hit him." What a small yet important victory!

When the Trip Becomes a Vacation: Well-disciplined Children Are Fun

Well-disciplined children evoke positive responses from others which reinforce their sense of themselves as "good" and likable. They receive more invitations to play and more rewards; as a result they experience increased self-esteem and self-control. These children are easy to live with, and fun to be around. They have learned to expect that others will like them and that they can have mutually rewarding interactions with others.

Positive Effects for Parents

Not only is effective parenting easier in the long run and beneficial for kids, it is also good for parents. Effective parenting produces these advantages: **parenting becomes enjoyable; parents see the positive outcome to setting limits; adolescence goes more smoothly;** and **parents help children to cope better.**

Traveling Can Be Fun: Parenting Is Enjoyable

As parents learn to manage their children's behavior, they become more confident of their parenting abilities. Thoughtful and consistent management of their children reduces or eliminates the need to threaten or belittle their children in order to control them. More often than not, their relationship with their children is pleasurable, even fun. Mutually rewarding interactions between parent and child become the rule rather than the exception.

Steering and Braking Are Better than Crashing: Parents can Overcome Their Guilt about Setting Limits and Following Through with Behavioral Consequences

As parents understand the importance of setting limits for healthy children, they do so more easily, following through with the behavioral consequences necessary for teaching their children self-control. If this process is begun early in a child's development, the need to establish those limits diminishes as the child gets older. Even though you may feel guilty at first, if you can set limits and follow through, seeing the positive effects of this strategy will help you to feel better about enforcing limits and consequences.

Even the Rough Spots in the Road Are Not That Bad: Parents Can Survive Their Children's Adolescence with Minimum Conflict

When parents practice effective parenting early in their children's lives, they begin to build a good relationship with their children. Children's trust grows as they realize that their parents will actually do what they say they will do. Such interaction provides the basis for a mutually satisfying, reciprocal relationship when the child reaches adolescence. During this traditionally stormy period, parents who have practiced the techniques outlined in this book find it easier to learn to trust their children just as their children trust them.

Detours Won't Wreck the Car:
Parents Can Let Children Experience the Natural Consequences of Their Actions with the Confidence That the Children Can Cope

When parents consistently set careful limits according to the developmental level of their children, they develop confidence that their children can handle and benefit from experiencing the consequences of their own behavior. Even more importantly, other significant adults and peers can take over some of the responsibility of limit-setting that was previously the exclusive domain of the parents. This transition allows the parent to become more of a friend to the older adolescent.

As we have said, we think the toughest challenge of parenting is to turn your child into your friend. When your children reach their early twenties, they will no longer need a parent in the same way as in earlier years. So, in order to maintain a good relationship, parents must be able to trust, respect and admire their adult children just as they do their other adult friends. We believe that our approach can create the conditions which will allow such a relationship to evolve, and that the rewards are well worth the effort.

We hope that by our pointing out some of the roadblocks to development, parents can begin to take them down. Roadblocks are frustrating for both parents and children, complicating the already difficult job of parenting. We are sure that parents want to make the journey of development as pleasant as possible for their children. We hope this book can help guide you through the most challenging and rewarding of all trips.

References

Adler, A. (1964). *Social interest*. New York: Capricorn.

Ainsworth, M.D., Blehar, M.C., Waters, E., & Wall, S. (1978). *Patterns of Attachment: A psychological study of the strange situation*. Hillsdale, NJ: Erlbaum.

Anastasi, A. (1976). *Psychological testing* (4th ed.). New York: MacMillan.

Anisfeld, M. (1984). *Language development from birth to three*. Hillsdale, NJ: Erlbaum.

Altrocchi, J. (1980). *Abnormal behavior*. New York: Harcourt, Brace, Jovanovich.

Bandura, A. (1962). Social learning through imitation. In M. R. Jones (Ed.), *Nebraska symposium on motivation: 1962* (pp. 211-269). Lincoln: University of Nebraska Press.

Bandura, A. (1965). Vicarious processes: A case of no-trial learning. In L. Berkowitz (Ed.), *Advances in experimental social psychology* (Vol 2), New York: Academic, pp. 1-55.

Bandura, A. (1969). *Principles of behavior modification*. New York: Holt, Rinehart & Winston.

Bandura, A. (1969). Social learning of moral judgments. *Journal of personality and social psychology. 11*, 275-279.

Bandura, A. (1977). *Social learning theory*. Englewood Cliffs, NJ: Prentice-Hall.

Bandura, A., & Walters, R.H. (1963). *Social learning and personality development*. New York: Holt, Rinehart & Winston.

Belsky, J., & Nezworski, T. (Eds.) (1988). *Clinical implications of attachment*. Hillsdale, NJ: Erlbaum.

Bergin, A.E., & Garfield, S.L. (Eds.) (1971). *Handbook of psychotherapy and behavior change: An empirical analysis*. New York: John Wiley.

Bergin, A.E., & Strupp, H.H. (1970). New directions in Psychotherapy research. *Journal of abnormal psychology. 76*, 13-26.

Berk, L.E. (1989). *Child development*. Boston: Allyn and Bacon.

Bettelheim, B. (1967). *The empty fortress*. New York: Free Press, 1967.

Bettelheim, B. (1970). *The children of the dream.* New York: Macmillan.

Bettelheim, B. (1977). *The uses of enchantment: The meaning and importance of fairy tales.* New York: Vintage.

Bettelheim, B. (1987). *A good enough parent: A book on child-rearing.* New York: Knopf.

Bijou, S.W., & Baer, D.M. (1961). *Child development: volume 1: A systematic and empirical theory.* New York: Appleton-Century-Crofts.

Bolles, R.C. (1972). Reinforcement, expectancy, and learning. *Psychological review. 79,* 394-409.

Brazelton, T.B., School, M.L., & Robey, J.S. (1966). Visual responses in the newborn. *Pediatrics. 37,* 284-290.

Brazelton, T.B. (1974). *Toddlers and parents: A declaration of independence.* New York: Delta.

Brazelton, T.B. (1983). *Infants and mothers: Differences in development* (rev. ed.). New York: Delta/Seymour Lawrence.

Brazelton, T.B. (1987). *What every baby knows.* New York: Ballantine.

Chess, S. (1967). Healthy responses, development disturbances, and stress or reactive disorders: I. Infancy and childhood. In A.M. Freedman & H.I. Kaplan (Eds.), *Comprehensive textbook of psychiatry.* Baltimore: Williams & Wilkins.

Chomsky, N. (1959). Review of Skinner's Verbal behavior. *Language. 35,* 26-58.

Coleman, J.S. (1961). *The adolescent society.* New York: Free Press.

Dinkmeyer, D., & McKay, G.D. (1976). *Systematic training for effective parenting.* Circle Pines, MN: American Guidance Service.

Donovan, D.M., & McIntyre, D. (1990). *Healing the hurt child: A developmental-contextual approach.* New York: Norton.

Dreikurs, R., & Soltz, V. (1964). *Children: The challenge.* New York: Hawthorn.

Dunst, C.J. (1981). *Infant Learning: A cognitive-linguistic intervention strategy.* Hingham, MA: Teaching Resources.

Elkind, D. (1974). *A sympathetic understanding of the child: Birth to sixteen.* Boston: Allyn and Bacon.

Elkind, D. (1981). *The hurried child.* Reading, MA: Addison-Wesley.

Elkind, D. (1984). *All grown up and no place to go: Teenagers in crisis.* Reading, MA: Addison-Wesley.

Erickson, E.H. (1962, Winter). Youth: Fidelity and diversity. *Daedelus*, pp. 5-27.

Erickson, E.H. (1963). *Childhood and society* (2nd ed.). New York: Norton.

Erickson, E.H. (1977). *Adulthood.* New York: Norton.

Fraiberg, S.H. (1959). *The magic years: Understanding and handling the problems of early childhood.* New York: Scribner's Sons.

Frankenburg, W.K., Thornton, S.M., & Cohrs, M.E. (1981). *Pediatric developmental diagnosis.* New York: Thieme-Stratton.

Freud, A. (1946). *The ego and the mechanisms of defense.* New York: International Universities Press.

Freud, S. (1924). *Collected papers* (Vol. 2). London: Hogarth.

Freud, S. (1936). *The problem of anxiety.* New York: Norton.

Freud, S. (1949). *A general introduction to Psychoanalysis.* New York: Garden City.

Freud, S. (1949). *Outline of psychoanalysis.* New York: Norton.

Freud, S. (1953). *The complete psychological works of Sigmund Freud* (standard ed.) (J. Strachey, Ed.). London: Hogarth.

Freud, S. (1953). *Three essays on the theory of sexuality* (standard ed.) (Vol. 7). London: Hogarth.

Freud, S. (1963). *Introductory lectures on psychoanalysis* (standard ed.) (Vols. 15,16). London: Hogarth.

Gardner, R.A. (1979). *Understanding children: A parent's guide to child rearing.* Cresskill, NJ: Creative Therapeutics.

Ginsburg, H., & Opper, S. (1969). *Piaget's theory of intellectual development: An introduction.* Englewood Cliffs, NJ: Prentice-Hall.

Ginott, H.G. (1965). *Between parent and child: New solutions to old problems.* New York: Avon.

Gordon, T. (1970). *Parent effectiveness training.* New York: Wyden.

Gordon, T. (1974). *Teacher effectiveness training.* New York: McKay.

Green, C. (1984). *Toddler taming: A survival guide for parents.* New York: Fawcett Columbine.

Greenspan, S., and Greenspan, N.T. (1986). *First feelings: Milestones in the emotional development of your baby and child.* New York: Penguin.

Guntrip, H. (1971). *Psychoanalytic theory, therapy, and the self.* New York: Basic.

Hallahan, D.P., & Kauffman, J.M. (1978). *Exceptional children: Introduction to special education.* Englewood Cliffs, NJ: Prentice-Hall.

Ilg, F.L., Ames, L.B., & Baker, S.M. (1981). *Child behavior* (rev. ed.). New York: Harper & Row.

Kaplan, L.J. (1984). *Adolescence: The farewell to childhood.* New York: Simon & Schuster.

Leach, Penelope. (1989). *Your baby and child: From birth to age five* (rev ed.). New York: Knopf.

Lindemann, E. (1944). Symptomatology and management of acute grief. *American journal of psychiatry. 101,* 141-148.

Lovaas, O.I. (1967). A behavior therapy approach to the treatment of childhood schizophrenia. In J. Hill (Ed.), *Minnesota symposium on child psychology.* Minneapolis: University of Minnesota Press.

Lovaas, O.I. (1977). *The autistic child: Language and development through behavior modification.* New York: Irvington.

Lovaas, O.I., Berberich, J.P., Perloff, B.F., & Schaeffer, B. (1966). Acquisition of imitative speech in schizophrenic children. *Science. 151,* 705-707.

Lovaas, O.I., Freitag, G., Gold, V.J., & Kassorla, I.C. (1965). Experimental studies in childhood schizophrenia: Analysis of self-destructive behavior. *Journal of experimental psychology.* 2, 67-84.

Lovaas, O.I., Koegel, R., Simmons, J.Q., & Long, J.S. (1973). Some generalization and follow-up measures on autistic children in behavior therapy. *Journal of applied behavior analysis. 6,* 131-166.

Lovaas, O.I., & Newsom, C.D. (1976). Behavior modification with psychotic children. In H. Leitenberg (Ed.), *Handbook of Behavior modification and behavior therapy.* Englewood Cliffs, NJ: Prentice-Hall.

Lovaas, O.I., Schreibman, L., & Koegel, R. (1974). A behavior modification approach to the treatment of autistic children. *Journal of autism and childhood schizophrenia. 4,* 111-129.

Maier, H.W. (1969). *Three theories of child development: The contributions of Erikson, Piaget, and Sears, and their applications.* New York: Harper & Row.

Marion, M. (1987). *Guidance of young children* (2nd ed.). Columbus, OH: Merrill.

Mead, D.E. (1976). *Six approaches to childrearing.* Provo, UT: Brigham Young University Press.

Miller, N.E., & Dollard, J. (1941). *Social learning and imitation.* New Haven: Yale University Press.

Mussen, P.H., Conger, J.J., & Kagan, J. (1969). *Child development and personality* (4th ed.). New York: Harper & Row.

Patterson, G.R. (1975). *Families*. Champaign, IL: Research Press.

Patterson, G.R. (1977). *Living with children* (rev. ed). Champaign, IL: Research Press.

Patterson, G.R., Littman, R.A., & Hinsey, W.C. (1964). Parental effectiveness as reinforcers in the laboratory and its relation to child rearing practices and child adjustment in the classroom. *Journal of personality*. 32, 180-199.

Piaget, J. (1952). *The origins of intelligence in children*. New York: International Universities Press.

Piaget, J. (1970). Piaget's Theory. In P. Mussen (Ed.), *Carmichael's manual of child psychology* (Vol. 1). New York: Wiley, pp. 703-732.

Piaget, J. (1981). *Intelligence and affectivity: Their relationship during child development*. Palo Alto, CA: Annual Reviews.

Piaget, J.(1983). Piaget's Theory. In P. Mussen (Ed.), *Handbook of child psychology* (Vol. 1). New York: Wiley, pp. 103-128.

Powell, M.L. (1981). *Assessment and management of developmental changes and problems in children* (2nd ed.). St. Louis: Mosby.

Rogers, C. (1961). *On becoming a person*. Boston: Houghton-Mifflin.

Salvia, J., & Ysseldyke, J.E. (1978). *Assessment in special and remedial education*. Boston: Houghton Mifflin.

Schultz, D. (1976). *Theories of personality*. Monterey, CA: Brooks/Cole.

Silver, L.B. (1984). *The misunderstood child: A guide for parents of learning disabled children*. New York: McGraw-Hill.

Skinner, B.F. (1938). *The behavior of organisms*. New York: Appleton-Century-Crofts.

Skinner, B.F. (1951). How to teach animals. *Scientific American. 185*, 26-29.

Skinner, B.F. (1953). *Science and human behavior*. New York: MacMillan.

Staats, A.W. (1968). *Learning, lanquage, and cognition*. New York: Holt, Rinehart & Winston.

Stern, D.N. (1985). *The interpersonal world of the infant: A view from psychoanalysis and developmental psychology*. New York: Basic.

Terecki, S. (1989). *The difficult child* (rev. ed.). New York: Bantam.

Thomas, A., & Chess, S. (1977). *Temperament and development*. New York: Brunner/Mazel.

Vail, P.L. (1979). *The world of the gifted child*. New York: Walker.

Viorst, J. (1986). *Necessary losses*. New York: Simon and Schuster.

Watson, J.B. (1958). *Behaviorism* (rev. ed.). Chicago: University of Chicago Press.

Winnicott, D.W. (1988). *Babies and their mothers.* Reading, MA: Addison-Wesley.

About the Authors

Mary Ann Little, Ph.D. is a clinical psychologist with a wide ranging practice. She received a B.A. from Smith College and a Ph.D. from the University of Texas Southwestern Medical Center at Dallas. She also spent a year of post-doctoral study in Piagetian psychology at the University of Geneva under the direction of Barbel Inhelder.

She has worked extensively providing consultation to hospitals and schools and lectures frequently on child development and parenting. In television interviews, she has provided information on children, child rearing practices, and child management. Her column, "Especially for Kids," published in the *Dallas Times Herald,* further looked at children's problems from a developmental perspective.

Dr. Little has held an adjunct faculty appointment at the University of Texas at Dallas and is a clinical supervisor for the Graduate Program in Clinical Psychology at Southwestern Medical Center.

Kevin W. Karlson, J.D., Ph.D. is a forensic and clinical psychologist specializing in trial psychology. He received a Ph.D. in clinical psychology from the University of Texas Southwestern Medical Center at Dallas and a J.D. from Southern Methodist University School of Law. He has held adjunct faculty appointments at both institutions where he teaches Forensic Psychology and Psychiatric and Psychological Evidence. He is a contributing author to *Psychiatric and Psychological Evidence,* winner of the 1989 Guttmacher Award given by the American Psychiatric Association for the best book in Law and Psychiatry.

Dr. Karlson's practice involves consulting with attorneys about jury selection, psychological evidence, witness preparation and trial strategy. He also has considerable experience evaluating and treating children and parents and in conducting custody evaluations. He is frequently consulted by attorneys and parents involved in custody litigation for help in understanding children from a developmental perspective.